What do these stones mean?

Joyce Sibthorpe

A testimony to God's faithfulness

for more than 50 years

222 Publications

2

222 Publications
2 Wrington Road
Congresbury
N Somerset
BS49 5AN

British Library Catalogue In Publication Data
A Record of this Publication is available
From the British Library

ISBN 978 – 0 – 9561037 – 6 – 5

This Edition published 2009 by
222 Publications in association with

Timeless Teaching
Onwards and Upwards Publishers
11 Nightingale Crescent
West Horsley KT24 6PD

Printed and bound in Great Britain by
CPI Antony Rowe, Chippenham, Wiltshire

Cover Design: David Salmon
Typeset: DPS, Backwell, Bristol

Dedication

To my children, Craig, Joanna, Daniel, Coralie & Ben
who were all part of the journey

Contents

Acknowledgements

Over the years we have had the privilege of sharing our lives with many people – some of them are featured in this book. Thank you for your part in 'rubbing' against us.

Without my husband Charles, this book would not exist. It is in fact 'our story' and although he would express himself in different ways and possibly with a different emphasis – we are one and many of these experiences are mutual. Charles has invested much time helping me edit and publish this book. He encouraged and cagouled me, making sure that events that happened many years ago, were described accurately!

Corinne typed the first draft; she was constantly encouraging and amazing at spotting typos and other errors as she did the final proof reading.

Angela and Anne – thank you for your help in checking the manuscript. I greatly value your wisdom and personal encouragement.

David – Thank you for your cover design, your creativity is really appreciated.

Introduction

*"In future when your children ask you, **"What do these stones mean?"** tell them, 'Israel crossed Jordan on dry ground.' For the Lord your God dried up the Jordan before you until you had crossed over.....*"

Some time ago I was reading the account given in Joshua 4:20-24, of how the Israelites crossed the river Jordan on dry land. This miracle occurred as the Spirit of God cut off the flow of water, giving a safe crossing for a million people. The thing which stood out was the instruction to pick up twelve large stones from the riverbed, and to set them up in the Promised Land as a memorial of God's miraculous deliverance. God spoke to my heart and asked, "What twelve life-lessons would you identify to be your memorial stones?" And I began to ponder that question. I have known Jesus for more than fifty years and He has taught me many things. I chose these lessons as memorial stones. I hope you will be helped as you see God's dealings with me, and that reading my story will encourage your faith. As Joshua 4:24 says,

"He did this so that all the peoples of the earth might know that the hand of the Lord is powerful and so that you might always fear the Lord your God."

Think through the issues raised, and take time to make them personal. Ask the Holy Spirit to speak to you as you work through the "Make it Personal" section at the end of each chapter. Go to the website www.the222trust.org.uk and listen to the short messages which will add further insight to many of the chapters. Pray for understanding, for it is God's great desire that all people live in freedom, joy and victory.

Chapter 1

A Liverpool Childhood

I did not know God, but He knew me. This is what He said, "Before I shaped you in the womb, I knew all about you. Before you saw the light of day, I had holy plans for you." (Jeremiah 1:5 The Message) Kindly put, I was an afterthought, an unplanned baby, an inconvenience, appearing nine years after my older sister. I was born with a cowl – a covering similar to the sack kittens are born in. In the seafaring community of Liverpool, this was considered to be 'lucky'. In fact, superstitious sailors would pay a high price to obtain a cowl, believing it would save them from drowning! It did not save me, but the God who had plans for my life, did.

I was drowning in a damp, echo-y, chlorine-smelling, swimming pool; and all because of my impetuous nature. I just couldn't resist a challenge; I had an inbuilt desire to win and to get attention. A friend had announced that she could swim a whole length starting from the deep end, and although I knew I could only do a few strokes, I was ready for the challenge. As she swam to the shallow end, I splashed, took in water, and sank. I was out of control, bobbing up and down, gasping for breath; I knew I was drowning. My mind, which was crystal clear, told me that you went down three times, and then you took in so much water that it was the end. In those moments life rushes past, I'm not sure what of my ten years I remembered, but everything I had heard about God came with extreme clarity. I knew I was not ready for heaven, and I cried out to God, "I don't want to die, but if I'm dying I want to live with you forever. Help me come to you. Don't let me go to that other place." Strong arms rescued me, pummelled my back until water drained out, my lungs filled with air, I could breathe again. Looking around, I realised that I was not in heaven, but rather in Dovecote Municipal Baths in the City of Liverpool, surrounded by rather shaken life-guards, who once they knew I was alive, unleashed their fury and severely warned me never to try that again. Although all I knew of God had been gleaned from a mishmash of Sunday school stories and school assemblies, He had heard the cry of my heart. God knew everything about me, much of which had been brought to His attention by Miss McClure.

I met Miss McClure when I was six years old. I still have a Bible she gave me, and a storybook entitled "Greek Gods and Heroes", inscribed with her shaky writing "To Joyce on her 7th birthday." She had been wise to give me a book which fascinated me, but she also gave me the Bible; the book that she loved with all her heart. God had planned that my mother and I should be living in the same building as this wonderful woman of faith. Her eyesight was failing, she was in her 70th year, and she needed me to read to her. So each night I sat beside her, reading Bible passages; I'm sure I didn't pronounce the long words correctly, but she knew the Word and would listen with closed eyes. Every night she would be in bed waiting for me to come and read to her. I was afraid she would die as I read under the spluttering gas lamp.

Miss McClure was becoming a very significant person in my life. One incident stands out - she was taking me to Liverpool, for a treat, to see the Anglican red stone cathedral, and the beginning of "Mickey's tent", which was the derisive term applied to the now finished Roman Catholic Cathedral. Both are impressive architectural structures, but they didn't make an impact on me, and I managed to give her the slip to view more interesting parts of the city. I finally made my way home using my return ticket, not giving any thought to the danger, or to the sheer panic I must have caused Miss McClure, losing someone else's child in the midst of a busy city, with all its post-war perils. She prayed, and I returned home safely, as did she. When my mother heard the story, I was severely reprimanded and threatened with all sorts. She told me she was ashamed of me, but Miss McClure looked sad and disappointed, which had a much greater effect. I knew she genuinely had tried to entertain and educate me, had made an immense effort, with a train and bus journey, but only succeeded in losing me.

With hindsight, I now realise she was my intercessor, she cared, and before I had personally come to know Jesus, she had already been promoted to heaven. I wonder if she knew that God had heard her prayers. I'm sure He heard her complaints when I left doors open, abused her cats, and came late to music lessons. It was her gentle inner strength that impressed me, her consistency, and her love for God's Word. She just kept praying, and God answered. He always does.

I'm the youngest of three girls. Barbara, my eldest sister, and Audrey two years younger, have always been there for me, loved me, bossed me, corrected me, trained me, and in fact were my surrogate mothers. My parents' marriage fell apart after sixteen years of stress, wartime hardships and other pressures. My sisters remained in our family home with my father, and my mother moved with me to live in a small flat, which was part of the house of Miss McClure. I continued to attend my old primary school, but now had to walk, two miles there and back. On many days I would return to the family home to play with friends and have tea with my sisters, and possibly my dad, if he was home in time. I was then escorted to the No. 89 bus, and so returned to sleep in my mother's flat. During this time I became increasingly independent, street-wise, and mouthy. I was doing my "own thing", but this did not go unnoticed to my primary school head teacher Mrs Buckley! She had taught both my sisters and knew the family well. Recognising the danger I was to myself she moved into action, being wise enough to know that boarding school was the answer for me, and caring enough to take steps to make it happen. My mother was working full-time, my sisters were training for their careers, and I was rapidly growing up and veering in the direction of trouble. My family sought to do all they could to supervise me, and keep me under control, but it was a losing battle. Mrs Buckley, however, was a force to be reckoned with, and while she badgered Lancashire Education Committee, Miss McClure prayed. Their efforts succeeded and I was given a place at King Edward's School, Witley, a co-educational boarding school near Godalming, all fees paid and everything provided. It was a miracle, which at the time I thought was luck, and Mrs Buckley!

Life changed radically. I was an eleven-year old free spirit, who had spent four years carving out a life of independence - now I was being tamed, and I did not like it. Rules were meant to be broken, weren't they? Mouths were meant to express feelings, to say what you wanted, when you wanted - but not at King Edward's School. The process of enforced change was underway. My first school report contained words such as "audacious, ebullient, rebellious." I hardly knew the meaning of them, but surely knew the consequences; detention, upon detention, for what seemed such trivial offences. I was bucking the system and the system was determined to win. The enforcer of law and order was embodied in Miss Jennings, my senior mistress. She saw beyond the external behaviour to the hurting child within, and I am convinced she was positioned in my life at this moment by God. She also came from Liverpool, and was therefore able to use her local knowledge to connect with me. All Liverpudlians know that ocean-going liners need a river pilot to negotiate the dangerous channel on their way to the docks, and it was this parable she now used to help me understand my need of a heavenly river pilot. She challenged me to ask Jesus to come on board my life and help me negotiate its difficulties. I understood my need, my own inability to be good and keep the rules. The day came when I personally asked Jesus to come on board of my vessel and be my helper, my guide and my Saviour. God always deals with each of us personally, He is so loving and creative. He wants us to accept His help, experience His love, know His forgiveness and cleansing from sin and to have a new start. He gave all this to me, and an abiding sense of His Fatherhood, something I had never known because my human father had been unable to fulfil this role.

The rebel wanted to change, and did. The self-willed, headstrong, out of control girl began the process of visible change. The highest scorer in the detention list became the lowest scorer, and soon was absent from those lists. The heart had changed, and the external was catching up, altering more slowly, but very definitely. The labels began to fall off, and the new Joyce was emerging.

Make it Personal

Psalm 139:16 in The Message says,

"Like an open book, you watched me grow…"

You may have been wanted or unwanted, a mistake, rejected, adopted or illegitimate.

1   Thank God He had holy plans for you; He watched over your conception and birth – in fact, over every day of your life.

2 Many heroes of faith had abnormal starts in life. Moses was adopted by Egyptian royalty. King David was possibly the result of an affair – "brought forth in iniquity" Psalm 51:5. However painful your childhood - God saw you, loved you and watched over the plans He had for you. Why not thank Him?

3 Have you met the living God in a personal way? If so, remind yourself of the details. Who prayed for you? Give thanks for those people.

4 Do you need help? Those who call on the Name of the Lord will be saved. Jesus spoke to Nicodemus about being born again, having a brand new start. (John 3:5-8)

5 New birth means you are no longer on your own, but connected by Jesus into the family of God. Have you experienced this? The Bible talks about God being a very present help in trouble. (Psalm 46:1)

Listen to or download the short message entitled
"Connecting with Jesus" on www.the222trust.org.uk

Chapter 2

The Challenge of Forgiveness

At school life was good, surrounded with structure and an atmosphere of care and love, I was swimming in the right direction, part of a Scripture Union Bible study group, learning to listen to the Lord, and enjoy Bible stories. I remember a Bible study from James on the control of the tongue, and being greatly affected, knowing my unruly mouth to be one of my big areas of weakness. I was doing so well, but the moment I went home, I began drowning again. Not physically this time, but emotionally and spiritually.

I had returned home for my Christmas holidays to Liverpool …. and Albert. After my mother's divorce, she began a friendship with a man who hated me. I realise now that this loathing was not just natural jealousy because of the heart position I held in my mother's life; it was far more than that. Albert was a respected member of society, a county surveyor in Lancashire, and on the outside he was the life and soul of the party. He was also a high-ranking freemason, a fact which now brought a clash of kingdoms into our home. He was part of a system emanating from the kingdom of darkness, and I, though very young, was part of the kingdom of God. Not surprisingly, war broke out. He hated me and I him. He was jealous of me, and I responded with frustration and rage. Rebellion and antagonism in me grew stronger. "You're not my father", I would yell at him. My mother tried to calm the situation, and she would say, "Just keep the peace, please keep the peace; don't upset him." I was always the one who had to give way, which I resented greatly. Often she would say, "I'll give you your tea on your own. Come downstairs when he's gone out." I reacted violently to this unfair treatment, as in every conflict it seemed as if he won and I lost. He was very clever with words, and used them cruelly. The battle raged; I lost the verbal arguments, and lost the freedom of my home. It seemed that my mother preferred to please Albert at my expense, and ultimately I felt that I had lost her. In my pain and frustration I poured out my grief to my heavenly Father, and sought His comfort. It appeared as if I had lost the joy and intimacy of that relationship too. My heart was so filled with negative emotions, self-pity, anger, resentment, and even murder! What had happened to the joy, the love and the peace that I had experienced so recently? Was it all a dream, and not the reality that I had believed?

It was into this turmoil that my heavenly Father spoke, raising the subject of forgiveness. He told me that I needed to forgive Albert. He told me He understood all that I was thinking and feeling, but insisted that if I wanted my peace and joy to return, I had to let go of the rage. My response was, "I've done nothing, it's all his fault." I felt justified, but understood that I could choose peace and God's presence, or live with the cauldron of negative emotions that seemed to be multiplying by the minute. I was trapped, knowing I wanted the joy and freedom I had experienced as I had yielded my will and my whole self to God, but struggling with the challenge of forgiveness and obedience. As I was working through this turmoil, I remembered one of the Jungle Doctor stories that Miss Jennings had read to us one Sunday evening at school. It was about a monkey who had his hand in a glass jam jar. He was stealing peanuts, and his hand held a fist full which he wouldn't let go of, making it impossible for him to get his hand out of the jar. He struggled and struggled, but in order to get free he had to let go of the nuts, and then his hand would come out of the jar. The inner voice of my heavenly Father said, "Release the nuts, let go of the unforgiveness, the injustice, and then you can get out of the trap, but you can't have both. Forgiveness will bring freedom, or if you persist in your hatred, you will remain trapped." I seemed to understand the issue was not the right or wrong of the situation, but my response to it. I was now battling with God's Spirit and the old, argumentative Joyce was in action. I wanted to justify my position, to rehearse the unfairness I felt. As I poured out my frustration midst tears, I knew I was in strong arms, well able to hold me until my anger was spent. Yet, still the quiet, strong voice insisted there was no other choice than to forgive. After some time I began to understand that I did not have to like Albert, nor to approve of his actions. The burning issue was, would I speak out words of forgiveness and be released from the trap? Eventually, I was able to say to God, "I choose to do what you have asked me to do. I forgive Albert." As the words left my mouth a blanket of comfort, peace, and triumph fell over me. The circumstances had not changed, but I had; an inner strength was developing and Father God was pleased with my obedience.

As I reflect on my journey of faith, forgiveness has to be a key memorial stone. I started to learn about the battle to forgive in these very real circumstances. I was young, and yet God chose to confront this issue at the very beginning of our relationship. I have come back to this "choice" many times over the years by different routes, but always to that same challenge; in order to be free, I must choose to forgive. The people, the circumstances, the injustice will one day be examined before the throne of God. He will give His verdict on those involved, it is not for me to judge. The moment I choose to forgive, I escape my entrapment, and go free. I can then experience the love and tender understanding of a Friend who heals, comforts, and protects me from every evil plan of satan, as well as from mental and emotional torment.

I returned to school life with a story to tell, a lesson learned and a passionate desire to follow God. The next six years were full of change, challenge, and for the most part fun. King Edward's School was a safe place, where I learned much, and looking back, I see how wonderfully God answered prayer, how academically, socially and spiritually, I was being prepared for God's future.

God works in ever increasing circles. Whenever we have been taught a lesson we will continue to revisit the subject, and go deeper. I started to learn about forgiveness aged eleven, but more that fifty years later I am still learning, and building on past experiences. Some years ago, I was listening to a preacher who said that in his life he had seen a pattern emerge. Annually he would be faced with a major offence where he needed to battle through to forgiveness. One day he realised that these offences were like annual examinations. Each test passed, took him to a new level of intimacy and authority with God. I found that I could really identify with this; forgiveness must become a way of life.

Renata's Story

Renata was of German descent, both her parents were from Germany, but had met and married in Canada, where they raised their family. Her father was teaching at a university, and in 1939 during a sabbatical, decided to take the family back to his home country to meet relatives and see important places. During their visit political tensions were rising, and before they could return to Canada, war broke out, leaving them trapped in Berlin, aliens who spoke German with Canadian overtones, strangers not to be trusted, ultimately displaced persons. Because Renata's father was fluent in English he was coerced into working for the Nazi government, broadcasting propaganda he did not believe in, over the radio. His family were safe as long as he did what was asked. The family survived in a small flat under difficult circumstances, far removed from all they had known in Canada. The children were unaware of the agony their parents were living through, forced to betray their adopted country, and branded as traitors. They grew used to their father's absence, but one day their mother didn't come home, and no explanations were given other than an announcement of a funeral service for both parents. This left three very young teenage girls alone in a foreign land. Renata began to call out to the God she had heard about, but didn't know, and He heard her cry and helped her and her sisters. They were placed in a prison camp and somehow survived those terrible years. At the end of the war they were repatriated to Canada as prisoners of war, but viewed with great suspicion, both by the authorities and friends and relatives who knew their father as the voice of propaganda. Renata had many issues of forgiveness to work through, but as she did, her faith grew stronger.

One day, as a German speaker she was asked if she would be willing to show some young German pastors around the city as part of a reconciliation plan. Again issues of forgiveness and past hurts raised their head. Did she want to remember Germany and all the pain and suffering? Would she hold on to hatred, or let it go? Could she dare to be identified again as different, as German? She had worked so hard to be accepted back into Canadian society, but after much thought and prayer she agreed to help, and met the young Germans. Here were men broken and ashamed of what their country had done, facing their own fears with courage as they asked forgiveness for the sins of their parents, and their nation. Memories were stirred up, grief revisited, much forgiveness given. She found herself strongly attracted to one of the men, but knowing his future lay in rebuilding his broken nation she considered the cost of the relationship overwhelming and said her goodbyes with a heavy heart shutting the door on Germany and the past. However, God had other plans; He woke her in the night instructing her to go to the port and personally say goodbye to the one He had chosen as her future husband! There were many issues to face before she eventually married her "Prince Charming" and followed him back to Germany to face more pain and rejection. His family refused to believe that she had spent the war in Berlin, and had experienced the struggle common to all who survived the Second World War. Yet again there was the challenge to forgive – what a woman! Years later I met this lady as she sat in a meeting where Charles and I were ministering, glowing with the presence of Jesus and full of peace. I felt as if I was speaking directly to her, and later I realised she was listening to the English, not the translation. She told me her story. I wept as I understood the depth of forgiveness she had been called to give. Not once, but over and over again. At the time that I met her she was ministering in a prison to criminals, many of whom were condemned and serving life sentences. As a prison chaplain she was able to speak about the need to forgive, to get right with God, and no one could accuse her of not understanding. She had suffered much, and yet she knew God's amazing love and healing and an assurance that it was this task for which she had been prepared through her own journey of forgiveness.

As you face the issue of forgiveness, inside your heart you may be saying, "It is impossible to forgive. I cannot do it." However, whenever God asks us to do something, He gives us the ability to do it by the power of His Spirit. A few months ago my granddaughter led her friend into a personal relationship with Jesus, and immediately the Lord began to speak to this young woman about things in her life that He was asking her to change. Her response was "I cannot do it, I have been doing these things for so many years." But she heard God speaking these words to her and later repeated them to my granddaughter, "Child, you choose to obey me. Set your heart to obey me, and I will give you the power to do what I have asked you to do." I was deeply challenged hearing of God's dealings with this young woman, because I understand after many years, that this is always the case. What God asks of us will always be possible. You may have forgiven, and spoken out words of forgiveness many times, and yet there is a pain and an ache in your heart when you recount and recall the incidents that have brought you to the place of needing to forgive. Go one step further than forgiving; ask God to heal your broken heart. There are wounds inside many hearts which can remain infected, but God is able to heal things from the past as well as those in the present, and He wants to heal and bind up those wounds. Let him do it. Cry out to him, not only for the ability to forgive, but for your own heart to be healed. And when you bless someone who has hurt you, and you ask God to bless them, you release supernatural power. The Bible says that we are to bless those who curse us, to pray for those who despitefully use us, and as we do that, we release a dimension of power into that situation that can only be described as miraculous.

Make it Personal

Forgiveness is not an option it is a necessity. Understanding a situation can be therapeutic, but speaking out words of forgiveness will release supernatural power. Is there anyone you need to forgive?

Matthew 18: 21-35

1. Read this story and feel the emotion portrayed in it - injustice, anger as well as mercy.
   Note in v. 35 Jesus speaks of life without forgiveness as "torment".
2 You have been forgiven everything, every sin against God
   God puts our sins out of sight – Isa. 38:17
   Out of reach – Mic. 7:19; Ps 103:12
   Out of mind – Jer. 31:34
   Out of existence – Isa. 43:25; Isa. 44:22; Ps. 51:1, 9: Acts 3:19

3. What about those who have abused you, and who you have not forgiven? Take time to search your heart. Some things may be huge, and some unintended insults or offences. Some may need to be spoken about, others not.

4. The Holy Spirit will remind you of particular people or incidents that still hurt and need healing. The Samaritan in Luke 10:34 bandaged the wound and poured in oil and wine for comfort and cleansing - Do you need this treatment?

5. You may remember situations and have no feelings, just numbness, sadness, and shame. Forgiveness will release you into life. Find someone you trust to help you pray through painful, personal issues.

6. Teach in the home and church a culture of forgiveness –
    Be quick to forgive
    Don't let the sun go down on your wrath
    Keep short accounts

7. Forgive yourself:
    Stand outside your skin – and treat yourself with compassion, mercy and kindness, especially when you consider yourself to have failed. When you can see your sin and the hurt you have caused others, and maybe your shameful actions, there will be a need to forgive yourself.

> Listen to or download the short message entitled "Forgiving Yourself" on www.the222trust.org.uk

There are two books that I would strongly recommend. **"Grace, the power to Reign"** by Harold R. Eberle ISBN 978-1882523191 and **"Love, Acceptance and Forgiveness"** by Jerry Cook and Stanley C. Baldwin ISBN 978-0830747535. You can buy them from Amazon.com

Chapter 3

Freedom from Fear

I had always been aware of fear; in fact I had no idea that one could live without its hold. In my early 20's, I outwardly would have appeared to be a fairly confident, buoyant person, but inwardly I was diseased, and crippled by fear. How had I become like this? A vivid imagination, fuelled by ghost stories told by my sister didn't help; neither did her squeals of delight when she jumped out at me from the dark. It appeared like fun and games, but for me it evoked terror, nightmares, and torment. I unwittingly fuelled this nascent fear by reading totally inappropriate books, novels that led to further fearful reactions from which you escaped, but not without damage.

My mother was a very anxious person who had unwittingly transferred much of her own fear to me. She had been attacked and nearly raped as a young woman. Hearing about this left me with the impression there were bad men lurking everywhere, especially behind trees, ready to jump out on any unsuspecting soul, me especially! I had to walk two miles to school each day, and part of my journey was on a lonely road, lined on one side by trees and fields, and on the other by a railway line. I clearly remember this road, and how I would take a deep breath and run its full length, hoping that no one would molest me. For an eight year old this was a daily torture and fear grew. It was as if my heart was a fertile seedbed, fear was sown in many forms. For example, I was the youngest child in my family, and constantly heard adults talking about tragic events. I did not have the maturity to process the information or deal with the ensuing emotions. During the Second World War, Liverpool, the city on whose outskirts I lived, was badly bombed. I clearly remember my father weeping as he told of a seeing a mass grave, made to accommodate the victims of a block of flats destroyed in the blitz, and how there were too many mangled bodies to bury individually.

I began to have nightmares where I would be buried alive and I hated going to bed. Fear of the dark wasn't dispelled with the light, I often had to look under the bed and in the wardrobe to check in case someone or something was lurking. Fear may be described as "false expectations appearing real", and they are very real to those who experience them, not to be dismissed with words such as, "Get over it, pull yourself together, grow up." Those who have experienced fear will tell you, however much you try, you cannot obey those admonitions, because thoughts will have triggered emotions, pumped adrenaline into your bloodstream, and made you helpless to think or act rationally. There is a healthy flight-fear reaction given to us to avoid danger. We train children to avoid fire, matches, road traffic, water hazards and other dangers. This is part of understanding life. I am not addressing such fears, but rather the things which continue to cripple and torment, unless dealt with.

In my case, it was not normal for a married woman with three children to have to wake her husband during the night, in order to walk through a dark house to visit the bathroom. It was not normal to plead not to be left behind with the kids and the dog, when her husband had to be away on a business trip. It was not normal to listen for every crunch on the gravel and expect intruders. Neither was it normal to imagine accidents and death if her husband returned later than he was expected. It was not normal to hate going downstairs into the cellar without someone else with me, in case of some hidden prowler.

At this time I did not know that Jesus had paid an enormous price, not only to forgive my sin, but also to free me from all such irrational fears. I knew Jesus as my friend and helper, but I had somehow been convinced that some people were fearful and others not, and I was one of those who had to find ways of living with myself and fear. The church I was part of at the time never addressed this issue, so fear had become a familiar companion, always lurking to attack both in expected, and totally unexpected ways.

Change came in 1969. Charles and I planned to attend a conference in Ireland. I was longing to be filled with God's Holy Spirit and knew that the focus of this week was on how to receive Him. I had relentlessly pursued this subject, both by reading books and questioning individuals, and was desperate to find someone who would pray for me. It was not possible to take our two older children with us, so a kind and very reliable friend offered to have them join their family in a beach chalet at Gwithian, Cornwall. It was ideal, they loved Auntie Rachel and Uncle Ken, Dorian and Martin, and so we left happy children and set off. This was before the days of mobile phones, and as the chalet had no landline, we were going to be out of touch for one whole week. Shortly after arriving in Ireland I began to miss the kids and became more than a little worried that they would be fretful and unsettled without their parents. I countered these thoughts knowing the love and care that flowed through Rachel, having utter confidence in her ability to care for them. However, during the night fear attacked, I imagined death, drowning, awful cries, pain, and loneliness. The images assailed me, and fear drove out any rational thinking from my mind. I wanted to get back to Cornwall, to reverse the journey, and to leave the longed for conference. I felt I needed to go immediately. This was impracticable, but I was irrational, behaving emotionally, out of control, and was unable to be comforted. The leaders of the conference quickly realised that I needed help, and lovingly reached out to me. I admitted that fear governed my life, and what I was experiencing at this moment was the tip of the iceberg. Gradually all my fears and panic were laid out before them and the picture was far from pleasant. On their instructions, I listed all my known fears, and told my Father God that I did not believe they were from Him. I acknowledged that I wanted to be free of them all and would no longer accommodate them as part of my personality. I asked forgiveness for disobeying the command, "Fear not" given so many times in scripture. I listened as people gently explained that what I had experienced over the years, culminating in the present crisis, was actually the work of a spirit of fear. It had gained access to my mind and emotions through fearful experiences, but now was ruling me and colouring the whole of my life. These friends explained that Jesus had broken the power of the devil and fear by His death on Calvary, and now could set me free. All my life I had been held in bondage, captive by fear and now I was being shown an open door, a way out of the prison. They prayed for me, I received, believed and stepped out into a new world of freedom from fear, peace flooded my entire being, and all anxiety left. I spent the rest of the week in Ireland enjoying my newfound freedom, received the gift of the Holy Spirit, and returned to Cornwall a different person. The children were delighted to see us; they had spent their week perfectly safe and had enjoyed every minute.

Our house was still a forbidding place, large and rambling. The cellar still smelled of damp and disuse. But I was changed, and for the first time in my life I went to the toilet in the middle of the night on my own, knowing that I was no longer afraid. Charles had been woken so many times to help me, but I now woke him for the last time, to share with him my joy and delight at knowing that I was free from fear! When necessary he now could leave me alone without endless complicated arrangements, trying to find someone to sleep in the house while he travelled. We both revelled in my freedom.

I was excited to testify to what God had done for me, and soon began to meet people who were also bound by fear. One of our close friends, Pearl, was unable to travel by train from Cornwall to London, because she had a terror of water, and the railway track skirted the sea as it passed through the south of Devon. When she heard of my deliverance she asked me to pray for her, and was set free from the fear of water. Almost immediately she took the train journey something that had been previously impossible, and was thrilled to enjoy the views of Dawlish Warren, Torquay, and the South Coast resorts.

Another lady had suffered from agoraphobia and been housebound for years because of this fear, and as I told her how God had delivered me she asked for prayer. She had already experienced a partial healing because of the love and support of her husband, but the day came when she realised that she did not have to live with this fear any more, and was able to enjoy life to the full. There were others who were afraid of cats, and spiders, and dogs. Fear is an enemy that dominates so many people's lives.

Twenty years later, once again fear came knocking at the door, but now I knew how to dismiss it. I was at home alone with the children and had watched the late night news. A newsflash told me that a murderer had escaped from a local prison, was on the run, and that he was dangerous. A warning had been given that no-one was to approach this man as he was extremely violent, and we were advised to check on our doors and windows to make sure they were shut. Charles was away travelling, the children were asleep, and I was just about to go to bed. Our security was very inadequate, our front door could be blown open by the wind, and my girls were sleeping in a downstairs bedroom next to the front door. There was no other adult in the house, and old fears began to attack once again. I quelled the panic that was trying to rise within and spoke out my confidence in God's ability to keep us safe and in peace. I checked the door and the downstairs windows, made sure they were shut, and went to bed. I read my Bible, and the reading for the day happened to be Proverbs 1:33, which says,

"But whoever listens to me will live in safety and be at ease without fear of harm."

So I committed myself and the whole household, into the Lord's care, and went to sleep. Faith won over fear, because I now knew what God had promised. Fear will always have the potential of attacking, but you can dismiss it like an annoying fly, once you have a revelation of Jesus' power and authority.

Our boys, all of whom enjoy outdoor pursuits and extreme sports, were at one time rock climbing on the cliffs of West Cornwall. I had been instructed to meet them at a specific time and place following an afternoon of climbing. However, when I arrived, they were not there and the light was rapidly fading. Images of broken bodies assailed my mind. I had trained my children to listen to God, and not expose themselves to unnecessary danger. So where were they? I didn't pray (big mistake). I searched the area and made plans to call the coast guard; I knew that daylight was fast disappearing and with it the ability to search the cliffs or water. Fear now tightened its grip. I ran to the nearest cottage and asked the lady if she'd been aware of rock climbers earlier in the day. "O yes", she said. "They are now climbing at Sennen. They said you would be here about now, and I was to tell you to go to Sennen. They'll be there." I went and found them safe and well. Instead of being relieved, I was full of accusation, self-pity, and anger. I rehearsed all that I had gone through, only to be countered with comments from my sons, such as, "Didn't you pray?" "I thought you were free of fear." I went back to God and confessed I had not prayed, I had panicked and called out in fear demanding that God keep them safe. I learnt a lesson that day. Always ask God what is happening - then act. On another occasion in similar circumstances when they were again late for a rendezvous, I asked God, and He said "Be at peace, wait, they'll be here in an hour." We establish peace, not by the absence of fear, but rather knowing what to do when it attacks our minds and bodies.

We constantly have to guard our hearts against fear. Both my daughters have experienced potentially dangerous situations whilst giving birth. One needed an emergency caesarean, and the other had severe blood pressure problems. Both walk in a personal relationship with God, and know how to live under His care and protection. I knew the dangers during childbirth were real, life threatening, and frightening. However, we were able to battle against fear, asking for God's wisdom to be available to all the medical staff. As we prayed, we dismissed the spirit of death and every devilish attack on our daughters, praying for God's presence and peace to be with them and their husbands. The dangers were real, but God's promise to hold them in His powerful hand and to give them a full lifespan, was more real. God gave me a word from Luke 10:19, which says, "Nothing shall in any way harm you" That same verse tells us that He has given us authority over all the power of the enemy. We used this word as a promise as we prayed for complete safety.

Knowing your authority is one thing, but it is of no value unless you use it. I was recently walking along a riverbank and a group of horses blocked my path. In the past I have been intimidated by horses and I nearly retreated, and then I remembered that Adam had been given authority over all creatures, and so had I, so I stood my ground, and commanded these horses to move away in the Name of Jesus. They looked a bit surprised but they moved and allowed me to go past before returning to their former positions. I may be practising on horses, but recently I heard of a young African pastor walking at night. He encountered a lion lying on his path, and with only a bike to protect him, he commanded the lion to move. "Mr Lion, I am on an assignment for Jesus, and you are in my way. Move." It did, and he went quickly on his way. Later, when he recounted the adventure to a friend, he discovered that this friend had been woken by a dream, and had been praying earnestly all night for his friend's safety. He had been instructed by the Spirit of God to "pray, as your friend is about to be eaten by a lion!" Authority and access to heavenly instructions, what a combination!

Children have to experience life with all its dangers. Wrapping them in cotton wool will not help. You need to place into their hands the tools they can use to combat fear. Our daughter Joanna was at one time living and working in Bristol, in an inner city area. She was required to work shifts, which sometimes necessitated returning to her flat at a time coinciding with the pubs closing, and so there was the possibility of being molested by drunks. These are real dangers, so what do you do? As I prayed about this, I felt that I should ask God for two warrior angels to walk home with her, and if anyone as much as looked her with intent, that the angels would become visible and would appear as nightclub bouncers, tough and strong, giving a clear message "don't mess with me". One day whilst she was at our home, I asked her if she'd ever experienced fear as she walked back to her flat after a late shift. She laughed, and told me she had prayed that God would give her two angels and make them visible if there was any danger. We were amazed at how the Spirit of God caused us to pray in agreement without having conferred.

A friend of ours, Bob, used to tell of how he overcame the fear of thunder and lightening. Growing up in Scotland, he experienced many thunderstorms and he would lie in bed rigid with fear. His father, knowing that his boy was likely to be afraid, would come into his room, lie on his bed with his arm around him, and whisper "It's OK, Bob. I'm home. I'm here." No matter how fierce the storm, Bob would sleep with the knowledge that his father was watching over him to protect him. Our Heavenly Father has far greater resources, but the same heart of love for each of us. In Isaiah 41:10 it says,

"So do not fear, for I am with you; do not be dismayed, for I am your God. I will strengthen you and help you; I will uphold you with my righteous right hand."

In Isaiah 43:2 it says,

"When you pass through the waters I will be with you; and when you pass through the rivers they will not sweep over you. When you walk through the fire you will not be burned; the flames will not set you ablaze."

Make it Personal

1   Recognise the problem.

2   Make a list of all known fears.

3   Decide you do not want to live as a victim of fear any longer.

4   Ask God to forgive you for not trusting him and allowing fear to be bigger than God.

5   Ask people you trust, and who you recognise have spiritual authority, to set you free from fear.

6 Ask for healing of all fearful past experiences, and for "triggers" to be robbed of their power over you.

7 Ask God for scriptures which you could take as medicine in the process of renewing your way of thinking, e.g.: 2 Timothy 1:7; Isaiah 41:10-14; Isaiah 43:2; Proverbs 1:33

8 Remember: Perfect love casts out fear. 1 John 4:18

9 Fear often has to do with an expectation of punishment or fear of death. Hebrews 2:14-15 tells us that, "by His death Jesus destroyed him who holds the power of death – that is, the devil - and freed those who all their lives were held in slavery by their fear of death."

10 Meditate on the change in Peter, when Jesus told him that he would live to be an old man. Once the fear of death was removed, Peter exhibited the spirit of boldness instead of timidity – John 21:18-19.

Listen to or download the short message entitled
"Taking your spiritual medicine" on www.the222trust.org.uk

Chapter 4

Faith

Faith is the atmosphere where miracles take place. The Bible has many ways of describing faith; you may have little faith or great faith, it can be as small as mustard seed, but it can also have the ability to move mountains. It is a commodity that God loves and always responds to positively. Faith comes by way of "revelation" – the moment when you understand, and wonder how you had failed to see what is now so crystal clear.

At one time Jesus asked His disciples, "Who do men say that I am?" They gave Him some vague answers, but Jesus pressed home the question harder, making it personal, "Who do you say I am?" To which Peter replied, "You are the Christ, the Son of the living God." Jesus then said these words to him, "This was not revealed to you by man, but by my Father in heaven." This knowing was not to do with the mind, or evaluated with other senses, it was a "revelation", a certainty that came as an impartation from heaven. I think Peter surprised himself as he spoke out his confession, and in doing so, the truth of what he said became real to him, and he knew he believed. Faith was birthed in him as he spoke those words.

Philip was one of Jesus' first disciples, and he immediately went to find Nathaniel to tell him what he had discovered. In speaking to Nathaniel he says, *"We have seen Jesus of Nazareth, the son of Joseph."* Nathaniel is not impressed and says, *"Can anything good come from Nazareth?"* When he finally comes face to face with Jesus, the encounter immediately brings revelation, and Nathaniel declares, *"Rabbi, you are the Son of God; you are the King of Israel."* Two people looking at the same person, one only sees the town where he came from and the name of His earthly father, the other sees His divine origin and His royal destiny. This is revelation, it is like removing a veil, or having a curtain pulled back to expose what otherwise is hidden.

Just before Jesus went to the cross, He was talking to His disciples and suddenly exclaimed, "You believe at last!" (John 16:31) He recognised that something had clicked, the penny had dropped. When revelation comes, you understand in a way that you didn't before. The two disciples on the Emmaus road were walking and talking with Jesus, but their eyes were blinded. They did not see Him until He chose to reveal Himself. Once they realised who had been their travelling companion they felt like kicking themselves, because of their blindness and insensitivity.

Some years ago I was given a cross-stitch wall hanging with the Name of Jesus worked on it. It is in two colours, and if you focus on the background spaces, it looks like Arabic or Hebrew letters, and makes no sense. You focus on the other colour, and you clearly see the word "Jesus". Once having seen what is written, you can't understand why others, and indeed why you yourself, failed to see it earlier. There are people who see "Jesus", and there are people who see hieroglyphics. It's all a matter of focus, but it serves as example. In a similar way, faith is an ongoing and ever-increasing revelation.

At the age of eleven I had experienced saving faith. However, I doubt whether I had understood the process. I thought it was simply a choice or a decision to believe in Jesus. Years later I began to analyse what happened when I acquired saving faith. It began with a promise I had read in the Bible,

> *"To all who received him, to those who believed in his Name, he gave the right to become children of God." (John 1:12)*

I had read these words, and it had been explained to me that Jesus, God's gift, wanted to forgive my sin, make me clean, and come and live His life in me. The question posed was, "Did I want to receive Him?" My answer was "Yes" and I was encouraged to ask and to believe that God would fulfil His promise. At this point I felt nothing. I was encouraged as an act of faith to thank God for what He had done, telling Him that I believed what He had said and to proclaim that I was now forgiven and accepted by God. It was only as I did this that the feelings kicked in, joy, relief, and peace poured into me. At a particular time in that sequence, faith was in operation. I had thanked God for what He had promised before I felt a thing. Put in another way I believed, and later found I had received. In its simplest form, that is how faith works. God speaks, we believe, He then acts according to our faith/belief, and we see the evidence, and rejoice.

At the end of a series of evangelistic meetings in a church in Cornwall, Jim responded to the invitation to accept Jesus and received prayer. His wife Margaret, already a committed Christian, regularly attended St Kea Church, Truro. Jim would drive her there, and sit in the back pew, waiting respectfully to take her home. He was not a believer in Jesus; however, during this mission week he listened intently to the preacher, and was now responding. It was his wife's turn to wait, as he went forward to receive prayer. Yet, on returning to the car, much to her surprise, he acted as if nothing out of the ordinary had happened. In fact, he did not speak of this event until one year later. The same preacher was visiting the church and at the end of his Sunday message, was accosted by Jim, with this accusation, "You prayed for me twelve months ago and nothing has happened. I had no Damascus Road experience; there has been no change." The missioner posed a question. "Did you tell any one that you had received Jesus?" Jim answered, "No, I was waiting to see if He had done what He promised, and as far as I am concerned He didn't." A wise reply was given, "I am not praying for you again. Go and tell someone that last year you invited Jesus to be your Saviour and see what happens." He returned to his car, and waiting wife, and said, "Margaret, this time last year I asked Jesus to be my Saviour." And before he could say any more he found himself overwhelmed with peace and joy and burst into tears. This man, who was not known for displaying his emotions, continued praising and thanking God. Faith had been activated by confession.

I spent several years asking God to fill me with His Spirit, according to the promise of His Word. The first time I asked I was heard, but I was waiting for evidence before I believed. In reality, I had been heard the first time I asked, but failed to exercise faith in what God had promised, seeking rather for an experience before believing and thanking. Many people do the same, their faith being dependent on evidence first, before they will believe, but God's way is for us to believe and then receive.

In 1979 a small team of people came to take a church weekend in Cornwall. Colin Urquhart was the leader of the team, and the main speaker. The others were there as prayer support and for practical help. They were staying in my home, and I overheard them talking after they had been praying together before a particular meeting. One asked, "How much are we believing the offering will be?" Another said, "Remind me, how many have we agreed will be saved?" I was incensed at what I judged was arrogance and presumption, but as the team were staying with me I saw such humility and godliness, and a deep sense of love as they served and ministered, that I was intrigued. Eventually I confessed to them my ear wagging, and asked if they would explain, especially after I had heard them rejoice over the accuracy of the offering and the numbers saved. They explained that as they prayed and waited on God before a meeting, they would seek to find out what specific things He wanted to do. After listening to His Holy Spirit they would speak out what they were hearing. Colin would declare what he felt God wanted to accomplish as he preached, and at the end of the time of prayer, they would have "a place of faith" knowing what they were expecting to happen, not just spiritually, but also practically.

The team were learning to live by faith in God's provision. There were personal needs, and travel costs, as well as the support needed for the entire ministry. They knew there would be free will offerings taken at each meeting, so the team asked God in faith for a sum of money that they felt was appropriate to meet their needs, and then believed that it would be released to them, and it was. I was confronted with faith in action, which both fascinated and disturbed me. At that time I did not have such a revelation of faith, but asked the team question upon question, seeking to understand. They urged me to study the life of Abraham, the great father of faith. First, God made a promise, secondly Abraham believed against the evidence of his body and that of his wife's, thirdly God saw his faith, and did what was humanly impossible. Why the time delay? Maybe it was to demonstrate that when we keep believing in God's promise, despite the circumstances, God is faithful. I know that people look at this example and gain strength. Not many wait twenty-five years for the answers to come, but some do. It is recorded that George Müller prayed for the salvation of four friends. He waited many years, thanking and believing without results. Then two were saved; a third came to faith at George's funeral, and the fourth shortly thereafter.

This book is full of incidents that occurred because of faith. The longing of my own heart is to have my faith in God grow and grow, and to that end my constant prayer is based on Ephesians 1:17:

> *"I keep asking that the God of our Lord Jesus Christ, the glorious Father, may give you the Spirit of wisdom and revelation…."*

That I may know Him, that the Spirit of revelation will be at work in me and that I will see more and more of God's almightiness, and His ability and willingness to do the impossible, if I will believe Him. Faith grows by constant use, like muscles, the more you exercise them, the stronger they become. Conversely, the less you use them, the weaker and more inadequate they are. From the time faith had been revealed to me, I chose to use it, and so began an exciting journey, which continues to this day. I am constantly seeking to see God at work in miracles, signs and wonders, which should be our normal environment.

I first began putting faith into action whilst we were living in Truro. My daughter Joanna had developed unsightly warts, which were growing all over her knees. They were embarrassing, and endless trips to the doctor who prescribed creams and medications, all proved ineffective. Basing my faith on two scriptures from Mark Chapter 11, I was instructed to speak to the mountain and tell it to be cast into the sea, also to follow the example of Jesus who cursed the unfruitful fig tree, and commanded it to wither and die. I told Joanna that we were going to exercise our faith, and that I would speak to these warts as if they were a mountain, and tell them to go in the Name of Jesus. I told her I would do the same as Jesus, and I would curse the warts and tell them to wither at the roots and to be removed from her body. Jo was eight years old and eager to see the warts go. Three days later the warts were diminishing, one week later they were gone, never to return. We told everyone, and rejoiced in our growing faith. We applied the same treatment to other minor infections, and had the same results. We were learning to put faith into action.

We prayed for friends whose garden had been invaded by crows, the noise caused a constant disturbance. We told these birds to go in the Name of Jesus, and they left the garden permanently. Strange things were manifesting in another house, causing a freezing cold atmosphere, so in the Name of Jesus we commanded everything not in line with the kingdom of God to leave and not come back, and warmth returned. These were small incidents, but they encouraged our faith, and gave us opportunity to boast about Jesus.

Some things didn't respond, one of those affecting me personally. I lived with recurring cystitis, a painful bladder condition, and however much I rebuked and cursed the bugs that caused this, they failed to respond. I longed to see God's power at work in my body, I knew healing was possible, but for me it had been elusive. One day, walking in St Austell, I realised cystitis was flaring up yet again. I also knew that Good News Crusade had an office in the town. They were the local "faith giants". And so I found the office, walked in and asked if Don Double was available. I identified myself; he knew my husband, and I explained my need. With little or no fuss he rebuked the fever, spoke to my body, telling it to come into order, and it did. I learned that faith needs no religious ceremony, or particular atmosphere in which to operate, and that it could be exercised in any place or any time. My faith action was to overcome my embarrassment and to ask for prayer. Don saw my faith, the power of God was released as he prayed, and I was totally healed, and remained free from the weakness that I had lived with for many years. Forty years later I can date my freedom, from the time of Don's prayer; believing God was his trademark. He had greater faith than I had, and I coveted the faith that I saw operating through Don. Whenever I meet or hear of people exercising greater faith, I'm not jealous of their gift, but hungry to learn more. I love to read accounts and testimonies of faith working, both past and present, and I press on to become like Jesus, who told us to have the faith of God. Faith can be equated with risk. Peter had to step out of the boat in order to walk on water. It is in humanly impossible situations that God goes into action. God wants us to experience His power and love, and to be confident of His ability when we reach out to others in need. To be sure of His promises and consistency, and that what He has done for us, He will do for others.

I was on my way to take a Ladies' Conference at Lytham St Anne's, and having received the message that was to be given, I was intrigued to hear the Lord telling me particular things He wanted to do in healing and when and how He wanted to act. He instructed me to start the meeting with healing and to specifically declare that He wanted to both open and shut wombs. As I did this I was completely unaware of the fact that the lady leading the meeting urgently needed to visit the bathroom, as she felt herself loosing a lot of blood. She was menopausal and the treatment she had been receiving had failed to stop the bleeding. I was telling the people that God had asked me to open the meeting in this precise way, and that in His Name I was going to command wombs to close. As I did this, her bleeding stopped immediately, and she knew it. I then proceeded to command wombs to be opened, and to my great joy, two barren ladies were touched by God. Their faith was rewarded, their wombs opened, and both gave birth within the following year. One had been treated for cancer of the womb, and it was impossible for her to carry a child, the other believed that her child-bearing years were over, but still longed for another child. What is impossible for man is possible with God; when He speaks His words have creative power. I had never prayed like this before, and I was taking a risk, but found myself knowing with great certainty that this was what God wanted. I acted upon His word and He did the rest. He loves to see faith in action and never lets me down.

Isaiah 44:26 has become a living word to me, it says,

"I am the Lord…. who carries out the words of his servants and fulfils the predictions of his messengers."

Make it Personal

Read Romans 4:16-25

1 How would you describe what it is to have a revelation of faith?

2 How did Abraham demonstrate that he was a man of faith?

3 Are you familiar with the ABC of faith?
Ask, Believe, Confess – You first ask God, believe that He has heard and is answering your prayer, then confess that He has heard and thank Him for the result in advance of seeing it.

4 Can you recall a situation where you believed before you saw the answer to your prayer?

5 What specific things are you exercising faith for at this moment? It is good to have a faith list, keep reviewing it, and thanking God that He is at work. You will see what you have asked for.

6 If you have had disappointments and stopped exercising your faith, check whether it really was faith or just hope. The Bible says: "Hope deferred makes the heart grow sick." (Proverbs 13:12) Faith works, so hope needs to be turned into faith.

Chapter 5

Faith for Finances ... learning to trust

As a student aged nineteen, I was invited to attend a College and University Christian Union conference at Swanwick in Derbyshire. The aim was to strategise, be inspired, and to hear what was happening at a national level, and I counted it a privilege to be invited. I had been asked to represent my College, and took a job during my vacation to enable me to pay my fees and my transport there, but that left me with just sixpence in my pocket, and the knowledge that I would have to trust God to get me home! I had been reading Hudson Taylor's biography, and saw this as an opportunity to see if God would provide in the same way for an unknown English girl. The conference had been inspiring, and as it was drawing to a close, I was more than a little anxious to see how my prayer was going to be answered.

One of the main speakers "happened" to be a professor from Liverpool University, and I discovered whilst chatting, that he lived in Hoylake, a town very near to Liverpool, which was my ultimate destination. Towards the end of the week he asked me how I planned to return home, and when I answered "I'm not sure yet", he offered me a lift to Hoylake, which I gratefully accepted. After arriving at his home his wife gave me tea, and without knowing any of my circumstances, he took me to the local train station, and before I could reach into my handbag, he had paid for the train fare to Central Station, Liverpool. Next, I waited for a bus to take me to Woolton, my home village; I knew I could give the driver my name and address and pay later, so I wasn't too concerned. However, also waiting was a neighbour who knew I had been away, not only at the conference, but previously working on a children's mission in North Wales. She was very friendly, eager to hear my news and bought both of our tickets, refusing all my attempts at reimbursing her. And so I arrived home with the same sixpenny coin that I had when I left Swanwick. I had prayed, God had provided for me, and I was thrilled; however, on hearing what I had done, my mother was horrified!

I finished my college course, got a job teaching, married my husband who was financially secure, and began to raise a family with no real money worries, and so forgot about this incident for many years. While my husband Charles was working in the family business, I cared for our small children. We were also leading a thriving youth work and living in a very unusual building, which at one time had been used as a Co-op shop. One side of the house was our family home and the shop premises side now became the site of "The Loft", a young people's group which we saw grow from 30 to more than 200. I spent many nights listening to endless tales of joy and woe, as the Loft was often full of teenagers. Our family home was connected to it yet separate, the basement became an outreach coffee bar, table tennis and billiard tables filled other rooms, and the main meeting would be packed on Sundays and Tuesdays. It was exciting, demanding, and we lived from day-to-day without really recognising that in fact we were living in the middle of an extraordinary move of God.

Life was extremely demanding, although financially secure; and this was about to change. One night, Charles asked me to go with him to a meeting where Denis Ball of the Post Green Community in Dorset was the speaker. It was being held in a tiny Methodist Chapel at St Agnes Beacon. As we travelled the short distance from Redruth, we were recounting a famous incident that had happened some years before at this tiny chapel in the middle of farmland. The congregation regularly held Faith Teas, when everybody attending was asked to bring food to the chapel, first having prayed about what to bring. They believed that God would make sure that everything necessary would be provided without human organisation. Their teas happened regularly, and there was always a stunning variety of homemade cakes and normally nothing was missing. However on one occasion no-one had brought any milk. Had God got it wrong? As they were pondering what to do, a strange noise was heard in the tiny chapel garden. On investigation a cow was found. Yes, it needed to be milked, and the problem was solved. God never makes a mistake!

To our surprise very few people were present at the meeting, but God had brought us there, and it seemed the message had been crafted especially for us. It was the moment when God called both of us to leave our secure way of life, and to be willing to do and go where He sent us. As the invitation was given, Charles was so convicted by the message, and sure that it was meant specifically for him, that he leapt from his seat and raced to the front before anyone else moved. I followed but not before another lady had got in front of me, and so we found ourselves kneeling at the front of the chapel in this order, Charles, this other lady, then me. Denis first prayed for my husband, and as hands were laid on him, a bolt of power passed through him, and into me. The lady who inadvertently had separated us, moved quickly out of the way. "You must be husband and wife!" she exclaimed, as she too had experienced this electric shock. Denis prophesied over us, speaking out that God was calling us to full time ministry, and that He would make the future clear. He warned us to follow the Holy Spirit's instructions, and not to try and make anything happen by our own plans or effort.

We could see no way of being released from the family business or the youth work, and wondered how God could possibly fulfil his word. However, during the next two years many radical changes took place as God began to unfold His plan. In a very surprising way the family business was sold, and the shop properties were rented. For Charles's father and other elderly relatives this was good news as their income increased, but for us at that time in our early 30's it spelled the end of security and stability, and our adventure of faith was about to begin. We had recently been filled with the Holy Spirit and were full of faith believing that nothing was impossible to God. We closed our vibrant youth group and "gave away" the young converts to local churches. We moved house to a much more convenient family home, financially stretching our human resources, and tentatively trusting God to make up the shortfall. Externally we had the trimmings of wealth, but we were not making ends meet, and one day we opened the bank statement and found we were £300 in the red (the equivalent of £3000 at today's values). God told us that we must clear the debt without delay, and from then on we must always be in a position, that if God said "Go", we could do so, not having to say "We'll go when we've paid our debts." So we decided to live on whatever we had in the freezer or the garden until we were back in the black, resulting in some strange meals! The children thought it was great fun to have porridge for tea, with grated chocolate on top - better than spring greens and poached eggs! ! In every area of our economy, we chose only to spend what we deemed the 'bare necessities.'

Into this situation came Arthur, recently converted and just out of the army. He knocked on the door one day, announcing that God had sent him to us to help us dig our garden. We talked, and acknowledged **our** need for help and **his** for discipleship, and so he came to live with us. He was surprised by the odd combination of food we were eating, and we told him of our covenant with God to live on what we had until we cleared the debt. He disappeared for a couple of hours the next day, and returned carrying a big box of groceries, mostly tins. He told us that he had been living in an isolated spot, and this box of food had been left outside his caravan. He had been thrilled, believing it was given to him by someone whom God had prompted to meet his needs. However, when he came to live with us, he thought that we would have no needs. We were rich, weren't we? And so he had left his cache of food in the caravan, awaiting his return. Arthur's food supplemented ours, and we lived for some time enjoying God's provision and paying off the debt.

Eventually, the time had come for Charles to be released from the business and for us to embark upon a lifetime of trusting God for everything including all our financial needs. Many people questioned us about the future. "How would we live?" "Were we being irresponsible?" We were the subject of much discussion and chitchat. One small boy hearing his parents discussing our situation, was reported to have said, "If God has called them to work for him, then God will pay them, so why is everybody making such a fuss?" During the next two years we lived with friends on their farm, renovated two farm cottages, gave birth to our fifth child Ben, and found ourselves stretched in almost every area of life. We were living off capital and the generosity of our friends, but our common vision had not been clearly defined, and ultimately we decided to go our separate ways. We needed to move house and faced the prospect of no job, no house, no income, but God amazingly opened up our first "faith job." Charles was asked to become the full-time co-ordinator of a mission to evangelise Cornwall, culminating in a ten-day outreach based on Truro Cathedral, with the late David Watson as the main speaker. Charles jumped at the opportunity, he had the necessary skills, but the salary was a "faith one." We were told "We would like to pay you such and such an amount, but we have nothing in the bank, and so it is going to be a walk of faith." My heart said, "Yes, I trust you, Lord", but my head spoke very differently. In my imagination I saw starving, poverty-stricken kids, with threadbare clothes. I needed a specific word from the Lord to release peace and faith.

In order to plan the Mission it was necessary for Charles to visit York and spend some time with David Watson. We were offered accommodation at Hollybush Farm, a Holy Spirit centre, which amongst other things hosts a small fellowship and a summer camp, and had a reputation for radical Christianity, and for living in the power of God's Spirit. We joined their week-night gathering, and as the praise and worship time was proceeding suddenly there was a very powerful message in tongues. It was loud and sounded like a rebuke, and when the interpretation came I realised it was a word specifically for me. God spoke, corrected me for being afraid, and told me that He was fully trustworthy and able to meet all our needs. The tears flowed, I received the word and peace was restored and faith released. We returned to Cornwall and put that faith to the test.

We purchased an old vicarage in Truro for a very modest sum of money, were given a mortgage based on our promised faith income, and so moved into this large, cold, and uncared for house. We saw our faith being rewarded and were able to transform this sad old house into a warm, Holy Spirit-filled dwelling. It was soon filled with people, some just dropped in for a cup of tea, others came to stay. They were welcomed, and God provided for us; we proved Him to be able to "Give us each day our daily bread." God also provided skilful tradesman, who had a few days to spare, and offered their services. Others came and literally emptied their pockets as they left our home. Needy people also received prayer and blessed our household out of their material abundance. There was no lack, but each day was a walk of faith.

At a time when things were not very financially abundant we were asked to give bed and breakfast to an Australian family, a couple with their two teenage boys. They were part of an educational exchange programme, based at Manchester University. They had a house in Moonta, a coastal town in South Australia where Cornish miners had settled, and now they wanted to see Cornwall, finding the history so fascinating. During a conversation it emerged that although having enjoyed their year in England, they had experienced meat deprivation, and were looking forward to returning to Australia and some decent meat! Unbeknown to them, I had nothing in my freezer except for the chops from two lambs saved for a special occasion. Reason said, "If you use all those chops, that's the end of your meat, which isn't very wise." Faith said, "Bless this family, be generous." Faith won, and I cooked all the meat. And so it was that my household of fourteen thought Christmas and Easter had arrived at once, such was the feast. At the end of the weekend, as this family said their farewells and headed back to Manchester, they handed us a cheque. It was a large amount of money and the instruction was to fill the freezer with meat. They had no idea it was empty, but God knew, and delighted us with His provision.

We were growing in faith; I was able to trust the Lord for basics, but not for luxuries. My understanding of God's generosity and abundance was sadly limited, but all that was about to change. In 1977 we met Colin and Caroline Urquhart, and through the miraculous healing of our daughter, about which you can read in his book "Anything you Ask", we felt very connected to their ministry. Our hearts were drawn to his radical faith message, which we had seen demonstrated as he and his team stayed in our home. To our great surprise God called us to become part of their small community in Sussex, the Bethany Fellowship. We comprised fifteen adults and fourteen children, sharing our lives, we lived in separate family units, worked together, and ran "The Hyde." This house was a small stately home belonging to the Warren family, and was surrounded by 1500 acres of farm and woodland. This generous family had kindly given Colin and Caroline Urquhart the use of their family home and other small estate cottages. God began to send people to us from all parts of the world and all walks of life, people eager to meet with God, and to experience revival fire, Holy Spirit worship and miracles. News soon spread and the work began to grow, others joined the team, Colin and Caroline moved into their own house in a nearby village and the main Hyde house began to accommodate Leaders' Weeks and Living in Revival Weeks. These were retreats for weary leaders who came to this beautiful place where they could rest, and meet afresh with the living God. No charge was made, people gave as God led, some who had little could only give little, some gave abundantly. Our corporate faith was stretched; daily we would present our needs to Him, and daily He provided, sometimes huge amounts of money, and sometimes the widow's mite. It felt like riding a roller coaster, exhilarating yet uncomfortable. Our personal faith had grown, as we had seen God provide for our family needs. Now the Leaders' Weeks stretched us further; we had to believe for a team of twelve people, for the running of The Hyde, the cottages, the visitors, and much more. We sought to live an Acts 2:44 lifestyle where we shared all things in common. Every family had different priorities, some spent more on clothes, others more on food. Some seemed always to have money, and others always to have needs. Having five children with many needs meant a lot of prayer and believing. Sometimes we wished the bank account was full and we were living a more normal lifestyle, and then at such moments we would remember where we lived and the privilege of being called to this work.

One day as I was driving back from taking the children to school, God spoke a scripture to me from Romans 8:32,

"He who did not spare his own Son, but gave him up for us all, how will he not also, along with him freely give us all things?"

He then went on to say, "I have given you Jesus, He's my best. Now stop fretting about petty needs, remember the lilies of the field are clothed by me, and the birds are cared for, and I've made promises to you that I'll fulfil, so stop worrying!" "Will he not also along with him, graciously give us all things?" Praise burst out of me. I saw that He had given us Jesus, His greatest treasure, His beloved Son, and everything else was small in comparison. My expectation and my faith were growing.

A few weeks later, we received an invitation to spend Christmas on St. Lucia in the Caribbean. Charles' sister, Angela and her family were living there, as David her husband was working to develop the agriculture on the island. The invitation was a wonderfully unexpected surprise and delight, but it caused a very strong reaction in me. I was angry, tearful and the phrase "a right mess" described me accurately. It seemed as if a carrot was being dangled in front of us that would be snatched away before we could grasp it. I needed to talk to Jesus, I told Him that I thought He was a stingy God who provided for necessities, but not luxuries. He told me that He had unlimited resources and my thinking needed to be changed and asked me if I wanted to accept the invitation. We shared the situation with Colin and the elders, who unanimously agreed that we should go, and that they would "stand in faith with us" for all that we needed. We made plans; not only were we facing our faith challenge, but also the unspoken criticism of people, who like me, thought that God was mean, and that poverty and holiness were somehow connected. How could we justify such pleasure seeking? God did provide, miraculously, and at the last minute. We booked the air tickets in faith, we planned in faith, and saved all our birthday money and other small gifts. Just when it seemed the money we needed had arrived, God clearly showed us that it should be given away to meet another person's faith goal. God did not fail us, and we received His provision just when we needed it. He delights to give us our hearts desires and has the resources to do so.

Our children were encouraged to set their own faith goals. Ben, aged 7, gave his bike away to a family staying at The Hyde. It wasn't a very good bike, maybe a little on the small side, but the boys he gave it to thought it was wonderful. He then started to pray, and night after night he would thank God in faith, for his new bike. A long time elapsed and then a letter arrived addressed to Ben enclosing a cheque. It was from the family who had returned to their professional life in Germany and wanted to say thank you for the fun their boys had using Ben's old bike. It was such an encouragement to his faith and enabled him to purchase a long awaited new bike.

On another occasion, we were taking a conference in Germany, during March. We'd left England experiencing spring, but Germany was gripped with ice and snow. I was very inadequately dressed, had no warm coat and no stout boots, just a rather lightweight anorak. However, God spoke to a lady and told her to buy me a coat. She did not say anything to me, but tried on my jacket for size, and upon returning home bought me a magnificent sheepskin coat. The lady and her husband prayed to find the right coat at the right price, and the first shop they went to had exactly what they were seeking and at sale price. The first I knew about this was when a letter arrived to say there was a gift on the way, and a substantial cheque, which was for Customs duty and import tax. I'll never forget the joy I experienced when I opened this wonderful gift. It was so much more than a coat. It was an expression of a Heavenly Father's generous heart. If I had been given money suggesting I buy such a coat, I would not have bought anything so luxurious or expensive, as I would have found it difficult to spend so much money on myself. Every winter for more than twenty years I have used this coat; it is classic, warm, and still beautiful. It always reminds me of this generous couple, and of a Father who delights to give His children good gifts. I no longer cringe when people see me wearing it, although I do remember one person saying, "Oh, I can see you believe in the prosperity gospel." I just smiled, and told how it was given to me, testifying to God's great love and care.

Charles and I had made a commitment at the beginning of our faith walk to tell God our needs, and not people. As servants of the living God we can trust Him who knows our needs and has promised to supply. At this time we knew that God was moving us on and that we needed to leave Sussex and trust Him for a home and new base for our work. We were in Sweden at a summer conference in 1987, knowing that we had to move about six weeks later, but having no idea where to. Ben was with us and asked me where he would be going to school the following September. The fact that we did not know was causing him considerable anxiety, but we hadn't received clear directions as to the next step in our faith walk. In answer to his question, I found myself saying, "Would you like to go to school with your cousins in Somerset?" His face lit up with joy, and it was a moment when I wondered where the words had come from. But later they proved to be prophetic, and soon we moved into Charles' sister's house near a lot of boy cousins, and for six months we rented their house until God made it very clear we should stay in the area. During this time in Sweden I also wrote a list in my prayer journal of twelve things I was asking God to provide in our new home. I had no idea where that would be located. However, I was specific about an open fire, two bathrooms, good light, and a garden that doesn't grow weeds. One year later, after God had provided our new home, I was back in Sweden and found my list. I ticked every item including the garden that didn't grow weeds! At the time, our home Firbank was surrounded by fir trees; nothing grew under the shade of those trees except grass, and one part of the garden had been planted with shrubs, again weed-free. Isn't God good? The house we live in was God's provision, but it was still a faith challenge because each month we had to pray in the money to meet our mortgage payment.

During the next four years we saw four of our children married, and each time God provided. We hosted each wedding, they were all very different, but every need was supplied. We have learned that you cannot out give God, we have been 100% committed to God's purposes, and we have proved that He has been 100% committed to us. Over the past twenty years God has grown Living Waters Church in Clevedon, and so we have curtailed our travelling ministry in order to care for the people. We taught people to tithe, and as a result we have been able to give support to many pioneer works overseas, as well as support people called to serve the church in a fulltime capacity. At one time we received a letter from a couple who had faithfully supported us over many years. They felt prompted to ask if Living Waters Church was providing part of our financial support. They felt that the workman was worthy of his hire, and that as we had curtailed our travelling ministry, the church should be responsible for some if not all of our support. So for the last ten years we have been blessed by the generous, loving support of those who we have served. We are not a large church, but the income indicates generous big-hearted people, who give sacrificially. Our son Daniel and his wife Tanya now lead Living Waters Church, and Charles and I are free from the everyday responsibilities. We are now able to minister more widely and serve in other places as God directs, and once again we have to trust God to meet all our needs.

Not long after our financial circumstances had changed, a letter arrived in the post containing a cheque, which fully covered the amount of money that we had "lost" as our roles had changed. With the letter came an explanation: "We are not currently part of a local church, but we tithe our income to God, and then give as He directs. He has blessed our business, and we have been grateful for your help in times of need, so we send this with our love. Use it for yourselves or where you see need." Again we see in this new stage of life, that God is faithful. He will never leave us, and we will never see the righteous forsaken, or His children begging for bread.

Our eldest son Craig is married to Milena, from Bulgaria. When Milena was engaged to marry Craig, and preparing to come to England for her wedding, she was planning to get a good job to cover all her wedding costs. She had been offered a modelling contract in Italy, which would pay her in dollars, and give her all that she needed to buy the things that she would want for her wedding. Before she accepted this offer, she was asked by an Italian evangelist if she would travel around Bulgaria, and translate for him. It was a question that needed serious thought, and her mother was anxious, encouraging her to take the more lucrative contract. As Milena prayed, God said, "Trust me, and I will provide." So instead of working in Italy, she chose to go with the Italian evangelist, and work for nearly three months, travelling the length and breadth of Bulgaria, in the days shortly after it had been released from Communism. They were meeting in a small Baptist church in Plovdiv on the last night of this extensive tour, when the evangelist asked a strange question. He said, "Is there a sister here, who needs a wedding dress?" And everybody shouted out, "Milena!" Milena had not told him of her forthcoming wedding. He looked at her and said, "You need a wedding dress", and she said, "Yes", and smiling, told him that she was getting married after Christmas, in England, and that she needed a wedding dress. The background to this question was that a lady in his church in Naples who had spent most of her professional life making very, very expensive, hand-sewn, haute couture, wedding dresses had made a request as he was leaving to go Bulgaria, and said, "As my final work I would like to make a wedding dress as a gift for a Christian sister in Bulgaria. So find me the girl, and I will make the dress." And that is exactly what happened. Milena was to look at designs, send her measurements, and this lady would make the dress. It was to be delivered to England before the wedding, and I was with Milena when she opened the box that had arrived with her brother. With a certain amount of trepidation we looked inside; would it meet her expectations? We needn't have worried because inside was the most wonderful, magnificent wedding dress, hand-stitched, beautifully made. But apart from that, there was everything that a bride could ever need, including underwear, gloves, tights, and cosmetics. It was a wonderful surprise to see such bounty, like ten Christmases all in one, as we delved into this beautiful box full of the most amazing gifts for Milena's wedding. I love to tell this story, because once again it illustrates that we cannot out give God. She gave Him her time and her talent, and He multiplied that back to her by giving her the gift of a very clever seamstress, who not only made a beautiful wedding dress that fitted perfectly, but actually had given such careful thought to all the other things that she would need.

I would like to honour the many people who have been used by God to supply the needs of our family and ministry. You may be one of those people, reading this book and I want to say "Thank you for being obedient to the Lord." I want to acknowledge the many times when individuals have sent a gift to us, which has come at just the right moment in time. We are grateful to the many people who pray for us, without whose prayers none of what I have related would be possible. Thank you to those who have given us time; who have entertained us; who have given us beds to stay when we have ministered in their churches, and for many other ways in which people have provided for us and for our family. Thank you to those who have looked after our car when we have been travelling overseas. Thank you to those who have picked us up and taken us to the airport. The list is endless. We want you to know that we are truly grateful. Thank you.

Make it Personal

1   Recall incidents when God has provided in a supernatural way for you. Give thanks – Psalm 77:11; Psalm 105:5

2   Do you think of God as generous and abundant, or is your image distorted? Ask the Holy Spirit to open your eyes to see God's generous, abundant provision for His children. I found it particularly helpful to study Deuteronomy 26, and there are principles there, which are worth noting.

Read Deuteronomy 26

1   Take some of the first fruits, go to the house of God, and put the basket before the priest (verses 2 and 3)

2   Declare the Lord's goodness; remember what He has done for you. How He has provided especially in the last month or week (verses 5-10)

3   Bring the offering to the Lord.

4   Verse 11: Rejoice before Him and give the first fruits away.

5   Verse 13: Say, "I have removed the sacred portion"

6   Verse 15: Expect a blessing in the month and the weeks ahead.

7   Keep repeating this pattern.

Remember, Rejoice, Remove, Give, Expect blessing

Chapter 6

Baptism in the Spirit

Having received the salvation of Jesus at the age of eleven, I was encouraged to read the Bible, so as an avid reader, as with any other book, I started at the beginning and read right through the Old Testament and to the end of the New Testament. I read how the face of Moses shone as he descended the mountain after having spent time in the presence of God, and I was expecting the same to happen to me. After praying and reading the Bible, I would get up off my knees and look in the mirror to see if my face was shining. My unchanged face made me very disappointed. I read of supernatural acts of God in the Old Testament like Moses striking the rock and seeing the water gush out, Elijah raising a boy from the dead, and Jonah surviving three days inside a whale. In the New Testament I read how ordinary men and women, filled with the Holy Spirit, saw healing miracles and amazing escapes from prison. I longed to see the supernatural and was frustrated because it was not happening around me. I asked questions such as, "Why did it stop?" and never received any satisfactory answers. Moments after I had become a Christian, I experienced my own small but amazing miracle when the Holy Spirit directed me to find my handkerchief, and also began to speak to me in everyday situations. I have described this more fully in my first book "Can you hear God?" But I was discouraged by my teachers who told me this didn't happen anymore and that God only spoke through the Bible. Because I now wanted to please these authority figures, I effectively closed my ears to the voice of the Spirit. I did know the presence of the Lord, He gave me understanding as I read the Word, but deep down there was a longing for more. I could not believe that the Old Testament would be so full of the miraculous power of God, the early church so birthed in the supernatural, and that it would all stop. The questions remained, but I had to put them on hold, finding no answers from those who were my spiritual mentors at the time.

The years passed, I married, and then one day Carolyn, my husband's sister, came home from her college. We met her train and she asked to come to our house before going home, as she had something important to share with us. She had been baptised in the Holy Spirit, she had received a supernatural infilling of the power of God, could speak in tongues, and was full of the joy of the Lord. It was evident to us that she had a zeal and fire we had never seen before. The fact that her Bible was falling apart was the thing that convinced my husband above everything else that something very real had happened to her. Having been raised in a very conservative evangelical family, she knew that anything to do with Pentecostalism would be anathema to them, but she was intent on going into the family home to tell her father and mother of her new experience. She 'd come to us first to ask us to pray, and also encouraged us to search the scriptures and see for ourselves that this truth was bursting out of every part of the New Testament. My husband was proceeding cautiously, but for me she was a kindred spirit, who had found the things that I had been longing for since my conversion.

And so began my search to be filled with the Holy Spirit. Carolyn described every detail of what had happened to her, and of the group where she had experienced this mighty outpouring from God. I longed for a similar experience myself and cried out over and over again for God to fill me, with no tangible evidence. We often had visiting preachers and Christian leaders staying in our home and I would weigh them up, watch the way they were talking, and assess whether or not they had met with God in this way. Some most clearly had, and we realised the privilege of having men of God such as Arthur Wallis, Cecil Cousin, and Denis Clark in our home. These were pioneers in the move of the Holy Spirit in the early 70's and 80's. Charles told me that I was like a Spanish inquisitor as I would sit them down, feed them, and then bombard them with questions, and yet not one of them offered to pray for me.

Then God sent a young Anglican curate, Barry Kissell and his wife Mary, to a Church in Camborne, Cornwall. They very soon became close friends, and from the very first time I met them, I knew that they were in touch with God's supernatural power. They were our contemporaries, and we watched as they reached out in evangelism, operating with faith, meeting various needs, clearly being directed by God. Barry would bring his fledgling youth group to join our Loft meeting on Sunday nights. I spent hours questioning them, listening to their testimonies, longing for them to pray for me, but I did not know that they were being specifically restrained by the Spirit of God. They had been clearly told that they were to delay praying for me to be filled with Spirit, until Charles expressed a desire to receive prayer. I can now see that this was a word of wisdom. I was like a racehorse, pulling, chaffing, longing to move forward, while Charles was still working through years of negative teaching. I am so thankful that when we did receive the baptism in the Holy Spirit, it was at the same time, and then we were able to grow in the gifts and in faith together. I thank God for their obedience to His instruction to hold back.

The place where God met with us was in Ireland, at the previously mentioned conference, with Barry and Mary Kissell among the leaders. A couple of days had gone by and a film was to be shown that evening; I remember sitting and thinking, "I haven't come here to watch a film, or to chit-chat and just enjoy myself. I have come here to receive the Holy Spirit," and so I remember accosting Barry in the library, and saying, "Look, I've left my children in England and I have come here because **we** want you to pray for us to receive the Holy Spirit." He then turned to Charles and said, "Do **you** want me to pray for you?" And Charles said, "Yes, I do", because by now he also was hungry. Barry prayed for both of us, laid hands on Charles, who then in turn joined him in laying hands on me, and both of us received by faith with thanksgiving, what God had promised in His Word.

We didn't experience fireworks or great outbursts in tongues, but as Charles and I knelt before the Lord that night, both of us experienced deep conviction of sin. There were things we confessed together before the Lord. For me there were books that I had read, that I knew I needed to burn. There were activities that I was engaged in which displeased the Lord, and so with many tears our hearts were tenderised by the Spirit of God, and He was beginning to change us. We returned home with clear testimony of our experiences, which for me included deliverance from fear, and for Charles a new intimacy and physical sense of God's presence. The scripture encourages us to "earnestly desire spiritual gifts." We did earnestly desire to speak in tongues, and both of us spent time crying out to God for this heavenly language. God honours faith and persistence, and eventually both of us received a new prayer language from heaven, mine was just a few words, Charles' sounded more of a definite language. I just babbled away like a baby with my few words, believing that, as I used what I had, I would get more, which is exactly what happened. As we embarked upon this adventure with the Holy Spirit, we discovered a new dimension of faith in our lives. Needs in the lives of others which we had earlier been aware of and yet had no expectancy to see changed, suddenly became opportunities for the Holy Spirit to show His power.

Such as the young woman in our youth group who was deaf in one ear, and we said to her, "You can be set free from that." It was quite a shock to find ourselves speaking with such boldness, and then to put our fingers in her ears, and shout, "Be opened in the Name of Jesus!" Where had this come from – it was the Holy Spirit within, and it was a delight to hear her testify to the fact that God had opened her ears. We saw more miracles of healing and deliverance, God doing amazing things and of course the word spread. Many people wanted to hear in detail how I had been delivered from fear. Within days a crisis arose with one of the children in our Brethren Assembly Sunday School. News came from the hospital that he was dying with a burst appendix and septicemia. We did not know how to pray! We ran out of words to pray in English, but we suddenly discovered that we were being moved by God to pray in tongues for great lengths of time, believing that God was hearing our intercession, and that He would save the life of this young boy. There was great rejoicing as the news came of his recovery, but along with all this new faith activity, there was also strong opposition. A person said to Charles, "All the baptism in the Spirit has done for you is create trouble." To which Charles replied, "It may have created trouble, but I would never, never go back."

We were part of a Brethren Assembly comprised of Godly people, who really loved Jesus, but who because of the teaching they'd received, had totally closed their mind to the baptism of the Holy Spirit, and to spiritual gifts, assigning them to 1st Century Christianity. Charles' father was the leading brother in the Assembly, and was embarrassed by our newfound experiences with the Holy Spirit. He argued for his doctrinal position and sought to persuade us to abandon ours. He produced literature to support his beliefs, which was extremely negative and he considered our new experiences heretical – and strife ensued. The more he pushed his dogmatic literature, the more we argued against him. It descended into a battle of doctrine where we would bash one another with the scriptures that supported our case. This was not helpful, and soon the Holy Spirit clearly remonstrated with Charles and me and said, "You are not honouring him, and you are not living in peace. You must stop this behaviour, you must honour and respect him, and just agree to disagree." So that is what we did, and God made it clear that we should remain in the Brethren Assembly. We did not seek to recruit people to our beliefs, but many who saw how the Holy Spirit was filling our lives, and how our newfound faith was working, also longed for more.

Into our somewhat isolated situation, God brought us in contact with fathers in God, who looked after us and helped us. Don and Heather Double who we had been told to steer well clear of, became friends and mentors. Arthur Wallis who was living in Devon a mere hundred miles away was such a help to us as we explored the realm of the Spirit. Charles, who was still working in the family business, eagerly awaited the visit of David Lilley, a commercial traveller who had been labeled "the tongues man" by his father! And so we began to grow in our knowledge of the Holy Spirit, eventually asking Arthur if he would come and teach our interested friends and the whole of our youth group about the work of Holy Spirit. We honoured his gifting and anointing, knowing he was far more confident and experienced than ourselves and many of those who gathered were filled with the Holy Spirit. The time had now come for us to disperse the young folk among whom we had worked for about ten years. The Loft was to close as our season of leading this large and successful youth work, which had grown to more than 200 young folk, had come to an end. It was not unlike the early church in Jerusalem, when the believers were scattered, as we sent them back to tiny little Methodist Chapels, to the local Baptist Church, to Anglican Churches, and Brethren Assemblies all over West Cornwall, not because of persecution but rather a word from the Lord.

And so another phase in our lives had begun. Those of the young people who had received the power of the Holy Spirit, began to share what they had learned. We remained in the Brethren Assembly for the time being and sought to honour Charles' parents. Later, it became clear that we needed to take further steps of faith and obedience which meant leaving the Brethren, which you will understand was very difficult for Charles' parents. Nevertheless, they fully supported us when we left the business, as we moved to the farm with friends, as we embarked upon our first real venture of faith with the Cornwall Mission, and later, as we left Cornwall and went to work with Colin Urquhart. The years went by and they saw clearly that our life was fruitful and our children were following Jesus. Every time we visited them in Cornwall we were able to fellowship with them, they were fascinated to hear all that God was doing through the ministry that He had led us into. We were glad to see that despite all their theological questions, they could recognise God at work and although they never fully embraced our position on the Holy Spirit, we had fellowship and peace.

Having moved our whole family, including five children, to Sussex we were now fully immersed in the work at The Hyde with Colin Urquhart. It was like living in a hot house where growth is accelerated because of the favourable atmosphere. We were learning how to hear the voice of the Spirit more clearly, how to operate in the gifts of the Holy Spirit, and were experiencing things similar to those recorded in the book of Acts. The Spirit of wisdom and understanding, graciously revealing "hidden things that lie in darkness", in order to release men and women from bondage and captivity. In one meeting a word of knowledge was given "Abortion, and guilt", and to our surprise a man responded. He had years earlier forced his fiancée to abort a baby, and had never received God's forgiveness, nor been able to forgive himself. That night he was set free – Hallelujah! Charles began to experience words of knowledge through sensing physically where healing was needed. He would then accurately be able to describe where the pain was, and how it felt. One time he described a very specific hand injury, involving two fingers on the right hand. A man responded, who had severed the tendons in these two fingers in an agricultural accident. After prayer he was instantly healed and later that night praised God worshipping at the piano, which he had been unable to play since the accident.

Words of wisdom were given that cut arguments and left everybody astounded. In answer to a question being asked at a Catholic renewal meeting about listening to Mary, Charles reminded the people "Mary told the servants, "Do whatever He tells you to do" (John 2:5), "and so must we." It silenced any possible contentious argument. Faith was gifted to us, as we believed God for His provision, and also for physical, mental, and emotional healing. Tongues and interpretation became familiar, as did the prophetic use of scripture. The Holy Spirit would bring back a known verse, but apply it to a specific "now" situation, bringing clarity and instruction. Visions, impressions, and pictures all added to the rich way in which the Holy Spirit moved upon individuals, wanting to bring His power to bear on a needy world. When the Holy Spirit moved in Samaria it was reported that the city was full of joy. And in a similar way, it was during this season.

Prophetic preaching was life giving. A three-year old and a thirty-year old could receive different things from a biblical passage explained in the power of the Spirit. At one time Colin Urquhart was preaching on the Book of Life, in which God writes the names of those who belong to Him, and our three-year old son was playing with cars, given to him to keep him quiet during the service, not seeming to hear anything. Later that day we realised how much had gone into him by the Spirit, when he asked us to pray that his name would be written in God's Book. A way of life was developing, leaning on the Holy Spirit, listening intently for His instructions, obeying His wisdom and superior knowledge, and marvelling at the results.

The enemy will always try to disrupt the work of the Holy Spirit, he never releases his captives without a struggle. One day, Charles was leading a morning prayer gathering in the community. He felt an urgent need to take authority over all the works of the enemy, and place everybody in the building under the protection and the power of the blood and the Name of Jesus. As he prayed with great fervour and authority, there was a group of folk waiting outside the door. He did not know that at the very moment he had begun praying, a strong reek of petrol was smelt among the folk waiting, and a young woman fled to the bathroom, quickly followed by one of the team. That prayer had prevented her entry into the room. She had come with the express purpose of throwing a petrol bomb into the meeting, but it had started to leak as she waited, and she had tried to escape to the loo to get rid of it. Life is never boring when you follow the Spirit of God!

It isn't what we know that matters, but rather whom we know, and how intimately we are acquainted with Him at this moment in time. The early church lost their reputation; they were accused of drunkenness, unruly behaviour, and turning the world upside down. Pentecostals at the beginning of the twentieth century had the same opposition, but as they let the Holy Spirit operate through them, He confirmed His words with signs and wonders. How the church of today needs individually and collectively to experience a fresh baptism of fire, a new love for Jesus. and a demonstration of the Spirit's power.

Jesus told his disciples to stay in Jerusalem until they had been clothed with power from on high. His own ministry did not commence until He had been baptised in the Jordan and the Holy Spirit has descended upon Him. Receiving the baptism in the Holy Spirit was life changing for me, and today I see myself simply as a channel that constantly needs to be filled so that God's Spirit can flow out to others and meet whatever needs they have.

Make it Personal

1 Have you been filled with the Holy Spirit? When? What happened? How filled are you at this moment? Look at these scriptures: Luke 11:9-13, Luke 24:49, Acts 1:8.

2 Do you understand that "Be filled with the Spirit" is a command? In the Greek it reads "Go on being filled with the Spirit continually." Discuss this.

3 Do you speak in tongues? Have you heard tongues and interpretation? Do you want these gifts? If so, ask someone you trust and who has this experience, to lay hands on you and expect to receive.

4 What other gifts have you received? Can you hear God? If not, buy my two books "Can you hear God?" and "Is there a Word from the Lord?" They will explain very simply how to hear God.

5 Are you a visual person? (TV, Films, etc.), or Audio? (Radio, CDs, etc.) Visual people tend to see things like visions and dreams, audio people will hear words and perhaps specific scriptures. Expect both, but understand you probably have a bias.

6 Earnestly desire spiritual gifts, especially that you may prophesy. Do you prophesy? Look up what prophecy does in 1 Cor. 14:3. Do you think people need to be able to prophecy like this today?

7 Lastly, what ever your tradition of Christianity or theology, ask the Holy Spirit to make Himself real to you. Ask Him to fill you according to His Word, and then step out in obedience to His voice, and you will experience all that I have written about, and more.

Chapter 7

Faith for Children

I thank God for our children; each was valued, prayed over during their developing stages in the womb, rejoiced over at birth, then loved and prayed for constantly, which continues to this very day. We were not perfect parents, far from it, but God knew that our heart's desire was for each child to know Jesus, walk with God, and fulfil the purpose for which they were created.

It takes faith to bring up children. I have come to recognize how much God loves families, and desires to see each new generation grow in faith, even beyond their parents' achievements and knowledge of God. I have tried hard to impart my own knowledge of God to my children and grandchildren, and want them to end their lives having established a walk with God that is more intimate than mine. We have five children, each married to believers, each with their own children. We have sixteen grandchildren aged from seventeen years to seventeen days at the time of writing. Bringing up children is rewarding, exhausting, challenging, exasperating, frightening, but most of all, life-changing. It is God's way of turning selfish individuals into servant-hearted lovers, which is a painful process.

I was thrilled when I discovered that I was pregnant with my first child, but apart from the normal emotional and physical changes, I had to face an enormous challenge. Only a few days

71

after conception, without any understanding of the potential consequences, I had submitted myself to a series of bladder x-rays. My sister, a professional mid-wife, was horrified, and secretly revealed her fears about the harmful effects of such a prolonged x-ray to my mother and others. Fear was a constant companion in those days, and my early pregnancy was accompanied with sickness and excessive tiredness, increasing the anxiety. The Holy Spirit led us to pray for the 'bump' regularly, and we found ourselves proclaiming the promises of God over the baby as we waited for birth. It was only after I had delivered a healthy boy, that the full extent of my sister's fear and trepidation was reported to me. Forty years ago I was ignorant of the many powerful forces that could be at work, but God caused us to pray, and proclaim His love and goodness while the growing child was still in the womb. God's life giving words were neutralising all that was potentially negative and harmful.

On one occasion, a young couple who were close friends, had allowed us to use their home to pray for the deliverance of a very disturbed young woman. Before ministering, we first placed the house and all the people in it under the protection of the blood and the Name of Jesus. During this prayer time the Holy Spirit spoke to me and said, "Put the unborn child under my protection." I was puzzled, but obeyed the words I had heard, yet was left with the intriguing question, "Who is pregnant?" God wonderfully demonstrated His love and power, setting the young woman free, and as we left the house I asked my friend Di, "Are you pregnant?" to which she replied, "I don't think so," leaving me with the thought, "It must be me!" A short time later, Di told me that she was indeed carrying their first child, and we rejoiced over the knowledge that the Spirit of God was protecting those still dividing cells that were becoming a fully formed child. However, not long after this, Di was in contact with German measles at this critical stage of development, and the doctor strongly advised her to abort.

She refused, knowing that God had spoken so clearly when the child had only been three or four days from conception, and that it had been placed under the protection of the Holy Spirit. In due time she gave birth to a normal, healthy, perfect, baby boy - a very real testimony to God's faithfulness and much prayer that had been made on her behalf.

It is so important to seek God as to how you are to pray and what you are to proclaim over your developing baby. The story of Samson gives us a number of insights; once he knew his wife was pregnant Manoah, his father prayed, "Teach us how to bring up the boy who is to be born" (Judges 13:8), and a few verses after that we read the question he asked the angel, "What is to be the rule for this boy's life and work?" Samson's parents realised that from the moment of conception there is important preparation. Pray against weaknesses and hereditary diseases, pray for perfect health and strength. If your family has a history of short sightedness, pray for perfect eyes. When I was having children I knew only a little of the potential of prayer, but today I always encourage parents to exercise faith for the baby, while it is still in the womb.

When the angel spoke to Joseph about the child Mary was to bear, he said, "….you are to give Him the name Jesus, for He will save His people from their sins." The meaning of His name is "Saviour." The name you choose for your child is very important, and it will label that person for life. You have a great responsibility to pray and choose wisely. In the Nigerian culture the name is first revealed by the father at the naming ceremony, and it is expected to be prophetic. Recently in Nigeria, I was present at the naming ceremony of a little girl, Esther Joy, and was greatly impressed as the parents proclaimed destiny over her life. Although I did not have this understanding when our children were born, we were nevertheless guided to choose names that have fitted each child, and are thankful that God overruled our ignorance.

As early as possible we sought to introduce our children to Jesus, and each of them invited Him into their lives when they were very young. They all have a different story of their personal encounter, but each would testify that it was their own choice to receive His love and friendship. Every relationship takes time to grow and mature, and spiritual ones are no exception. At first their faith was child-like, but not childish. They knew Jesus was present in our house, an invisible, yet real presence. They heard us pray for them, and we encouraged them to ask questions, knowing that the Holy Spirit can bring understanding to very young children.

One night, when Craig was about four-and-a-half and bouncing on his bed, he suddenly exclaimed, "I'm not human, you know, I'm superhuman!" I was amazed at this statement. "How's that?" I questioned. Craig continued, "Well, as I've got God inside me, and He can do anything, that makes me superhuman." We may laugh at this "childish thinking," but there are some adults who have yet to grasp the significance or reality of such a truth.

Similarly, when we were baptised in the Holy Spirit, they were intrigued by speaking in tongues. "Can I do that, mummy?" I knew John was filled with the Holy Spirit from birth, so why not? They loved to hear me pray in tongues over them as they were being settled for the night. It was their questionings that prompted me to ask for the gift of interpretation of tongues, so that I could tell them what was being spoken. Don't get the idea that this happened every night. It didn't. However, we ourselves experienced such joy when we were filled with the Holy Spirit, that we wanted our children to enter into the supernatural dimension of faith as soon as possible.

Our children are all very different in personality. Some of them are more able to talk about their internal personal happenings than others. Never confuse quietness with disinterest. Ben had listened to the Word of God from birth, he lived in an atmosphere of faith, he was the youngest, and also at that time, less talkative than our other children. We were amazed when at the age of about eleven or twelve, at a young people's meeting he was asked what he knew of the book of Job, and talked about its contents in a way that totally surprised us. Where did he get that knowledge? Over the years God had been teaching him, although we didn't know it.

Our children experienced both the trauma and the wonder of Joanna's healing, mentioned earlier. At the age of nine she had been in an accident where a pot of molten lead had exploded in her face. Colin Urquhart was staying in our home at the time, and through prayer and faith her eyes and face were totally healed. Despite living with all the spiritual and supernatural things going on around, it was not a cloistered life and they had to deal with life in the real world. They had to forgive when they were let down by their school friends, sort out rows with other siblings, learn to share, not only toys, but our time. They had to make choices to be happy and overcome negative emotions and they were disciplined as well as trained to do chores and homework.

As they entered their teenage years we began to realise that new influences were coming from many directions. What peers think and do becomes important, and is not always helpful. As a result of our community lifestyle our children had friends whose upbringing was not dissimilar to their own. Nevertheless, each family needed to battle worrying behaviour, rebellion, and deception. When Craig was fourteen, he wasn't impressed with Church, God was OK, "But the rest of you lot are so boring." This, despite the fact that people from all over the world were beating a path to our door. One particular night we were on our way to a special Tuesday evening meeting in the main house, The Hyde. As Charles checked to make sure Craig was aware that we were going out (300 yards up the road), he saw some strange packages on his desk.

"What are you doing with that stuff?" Charles questioned.

"Making a bomb" was the serious reply.

"Just take it now and throw it in the bin, it's dangerous!" were Charles' instructions, but he had no time to enforce the command, and proceeded to the main house, where he was part of the team leading worship. The room was packed, as it had been for the past three weeks as Colin had been teaching on 'How to know Jesus, and be filled with the Spirit.' This was to be the response evening when those present could receive personal prayer. At the moment Colin was inviting people to respond to the message, there was an ear-shattering explosion. I knew nothing of the conversation between Craig and Charles, I had settled the younger children, and gone up to the meeting. Charles was at the piano, but trapped because of the crowd. As minutes passed and no one came to disturb the meeting, he began to feel easier reasoning that if any serious hurt or damage had occurred, someone would have interrupted the meeting. Colin continued praying, but then a police car appeared outside the building, stopped and began to radio back to HQ. The report was picked up by our PA system, and into the quietness the words came,

"We are investigating an explosion on The Hyde estate, over."

"A loud explosion, over."

"No sign of fire, over."

"At present we are outside the main house, about to make our way to the stables where the horses have become distressed, over."

"Yes, the explosion was reported by the owner of the racehorses, over."

"We are outside the main house, there appears to be some sort of meeting going on, it looks like a séance, over."

The police car moved on, and Colin kept on praying! As soon as possible I got out of the meeting, and raced to our home to find, what I thought, were five sleeping children. Minutes later I was followed by Charles who was not fooled. Craig was hauled out of bed, interrogated, and reprimanded in no uncertain terms. Colin too added his authority to the remonstrations.

It could have been disastrous. The bomb was packed into the detonating cylinder of a fire extinguisher, the children hid behind a shed escaping the blast, and thankfully the shrapnel was embedded, in trees, not people. But for us it was a wakeup call. We lived in a praying community, where we were servicing so many different needs, we were interceding for the nation and for individuals, for missions and revival - but our own children were not really receiving any focussed prayer.

A new regime began. The alarm was set half an hour earlier, Charles would make a cup of tea and we would sit up in bed with our tea and pray. God gave us a specific promise

Isaiah 44:3,

"I will pour out my Spirit on your offspring, and my blessing on your descendants."

Every day we proclaimed this, and other scriptures, over our children. To begin with we saw little change, but we were not going to give up. Within a year Craig began to open up to us, asking searching questions, and listening to answers which eventually led him to pursue his own adult relationship with God - no longer based on the faith of his parents, but on what he himself had discovered. This is an important transition, which needs to happen, but for your children, may not occur with such drama. Each child will need to move from knowledge taught by others, to knowledge experienced by themselves. Your believing prayers, and God's faithfulness will bring about that revelation.

The position of the father at this stage of life is vital. Boys need role models. If a father can worship freely and spontaneously, then it's OK for his son to do so. If the father follows God in a wholehearted unashamed manner, it will make it easier for his son. When fathers and sons do practical tasks together it helps create the atmosphere for men and boys to talk. You need to recognise they communicate differently from the female species. A father who demonstrates a consistent lifestyle, loving his wife and his children is modelling something that can be followed. He doesn't need to be perfect, simply consistent, as most things are better caught than taught. Mothers will spend the larger part of the pre-school and junior school years imputing into their children, but fathers are really needed as their offspring enter puberty and teenage years. At that stage, what dad thinks is much more 'cool' than what mum thinks. I remember there was a time when dad could do no wrong, and mum could do no right, but eventually the balance is restored!

While Craig's acts of rebellion were very obvious, another one of our children was determined to demonstrate her independence by doing her own thing, which led to constant strife and verbal arguments. One day, my eyes were opened to the underlying cause of this conflict. I began to recognise that during the school holiday time there was generally peace and cooperation, but as soon as she returned to the dominant influence of school, rebellion and general mouthiness again reared its head. I had been battling this with my will and determination, when God told me not to argue and fight with my child, but to recognise the spirit behind such behaviour. "What spirit?" I asked. The Holy Spirit replied "The spirit of the age." As I listened further, I began to understand the effect of this negative influence, which is so rife in our schools - rebellion, dishonour and the disregard towards all authority. Now I had a strategy, given by God's Spirit, and together, Charles and I confronted this "spirit of the age," refused it access to our children, and especially our daughter, and forbade it to enter our house. The result was remarkable, her behaviour changed almost instantly, and when occasionally it would begin creeping back we would reinforce the command that had already been given. Rebellion was not welcome in our home.

As our children were progressing through their teenage years, we encouraged them to seek to make decisions by personally listening to God. One of the key issues at this time was "Party-going." As each invitation was being considered and discussed, we would have several conversations, which went something like this.

"But everyone is going to this party, can't I go?"
To which I replied, "Have you asked the Lord?"
This drew forth the response, "Oh, I knew you'd say that."
"Well, have you?"
"No."
"Well, will you?"
"Oh, all right."

"Good, and I will too. I'm not trying to spoil your fun, but I want you to be safe." On one occasion I felt 'No' was the answer, and my daughter reluctantly agreed. She had also heard a 'No', but was finding it difficult to obey. But thank God we both heard 'No'. The party was gatecrashed by druggies from Brighton, and all sorts of horrible things went on, leaving several traumatised young people. God knew best.

One "faith prayer" we prayed from the time the children were very small, was this "Lord, prepare each one for their future life partner, and prepare their future partner for them." Our children all found their other halves, and married when they were relatively young, and so avoided the dating heartbreak so many experience. We had to trust God and give our children into new relationships that must now become progressively stronger than those forged with us through childhood. The

Bible is very clear that when a child is married they must leave
parental control, and cleave to their God-appointed partner. Not
easy when the new husband hasn't got dad's skills, or the wife
can't compare with mum in the domestic realm. Nevertheless,
leave they must. We learned this principle very clearly as guests
attending the wedding of Don Double's son, Nigel. When Don
gave his speech, he turned to Nigel and said, "Heather and I
have sought to train you, and give you a good home. We have
done all that we could to bring you to this point in time, but
now we willingly release you to be your own man, to be a
husband to Barbara, and to develop your own relationship and
family life. We will not try to influence you, but are very willing
to help, but only if you ask."

On several occasions our married children have come to
live with us, but we have treated them as a separate unit. We
released them on their wedding day, and even when we see ways
in which our wisdom might help them, we wait until asked for
help. We try not to interfere, but also not to be neglectful. They
will always remain our children, and our hearts will be towards
them and their spouses; but godly order requires letting go, and
letting them become a strong unit with God. Sometimes this
happens naturally because of physical distance. As we have
had children who are involved with us in the same church
and live in close proximity, it has been essential to practise this
principle. When you see things you don't like, or agree to, it's
better to pray. Pass the anxiety over to the Lord, and let Him
correct and teach them, as He chooses.

My mother-in-law, Mary Sibthorpe, was a remarkable lady.
She had four children, and her prime goal was that they would
have a personal relationship with Jesus. She prayed for their
future spouses, and I never heard mum or dad speak negatively
about any of their sons-in-law. I would not have been a natural
choice for their son. I didn't come from their religious or social
background. However, once Charles had chosen me to be his

wife, they accepted and loved me which I'm sure wasn't easy. As a northerner I was often too direct in what I said. As the years went by, I grew to love and respect Mary, and I honour her faith. She went to her heavenly reward at the age of ninety-eight, having raised four children, nineteen grand-children, and thirty-seven great-grandchildren, and those who are old enough to understand, are all actively following in her path of faith in Jesus. She didn't achieve fame professionally, or in the Christian world. She was content to be her husband's support, and run her home. But in my eyes, she was a woman with great faith for her family, and I seek to honour her and emulate her example.

Make it Personal

1. Listen to the teaching given by Joyce and Charles – Investing in Children given as a Teaching Seminar at Kingdom Faith South West, Taunton. You can listen or download from www.the222trust.org.uk

2. Are there changes you need to make in order to spend time praying for your children?

3. Some years ago I came across a wonderful idea – it was to cut out 'egg' shaped pieces of paper and write on each one the name of one of my children and a promise that God had given concerning that child. I then would place them in my Bible and constantly use them to remind me to pray, believing that like 'eggs' the promise would hatch at the right moment. It has been a great encouragement to look back at these 'eggs' and see God's faithfulness.

Listen to or download the short message entitled
"Eggs" on www.the222trust.org.uk

Chapter 8

Judging

My mother was extremely perceptive, and could "read" people with great accuracy. She had a kind heart, would go to any length to help her friends and neighbours, but was critical and clever with her tongue. She was from the north of England, straight talking, canny and sharp. I grew up in an atmosphere of blunt speaking, and although I learned not to verbalise all I observed, I often saw people's weaknesses and shortfalls very clearly. I expected everyone to be like me, quick in thought and action, and when they weren't, I mentally placed them into some lower category. As I recall this, I feel deeply embarrassed, but want to paint an accurate picture, even if it is an unpleasant one.

People who loved me made excuses for me, and I also excused my negative remarks by justifying myself with words such as, "Well, you probably think the same as I do, but haven't got the guts to say it." People who liked me lived with this weakness, and others kept me at arms length. Occasionally, I would go too far and hurt or upset someone, and would immediately be sorry and ask for forgiveness for my bluntness, but I never saw that I needed to change. I instinctively knew if people liked me, approved or disapproved of me, and like most people, was drawn to those who accepted me. Over the years I learned how to be pleasant to people, to behave appropriately, and in time, to put a guard on my tongue, having learned the effect that words can have. The external may have been controlled, but not the internal - I was an extremely critical person.

Then the Holy Spirit got to work, and as He so often does, He uses people and their own personal stories. My sister-in-law and her husband were taking a leadership course with Youth with a Mission, and had come to stay with us for a few days. As we were enjoying fellowship, Carolyn began to tell me how the Lord had shown her a 'bitter root' in her heart. She shared the scripture where it commands us to see "that no bitter root grows up to cause trouble and defile many" (Hebrews12:15), and then she proceeded to confess how she had judged so many people. In fact, there were few, perhaps none, who had escaped her criticism. She told me how the Lord had brought conviction to her, and how she was seeking to become a totally different person. I was devastated. She was describing herself and exposing a side of her character that I had never seen. I would never have described her as a critical person, in fact, quite the opposite. In complete contrast to my own upbringing, she had been raised to control her tongue, mask the external, but the internal problem was very familiar. I considered on a range of naught to ten, she was probably a 'two or three' and I was certainly a 'ten'. If she needed the Holy Spirit to help her, then what about me?

Once a problem has been exposed, I'm usually quick to deal with it, especially when it concerns my relationship with God. So I went to prayer, and soon realised that God wanted to deliver me from my own root of bitterness, much of which had been learned behaviour, but it still had the power to defile many. To make this exercise totally practical, I decided to take a telephone list of the people in the fellowship where I was living, and to ask myself honestly, "Had I been critical of them?" I was horrified as I recalled thoughts and words spoken that exposed the evil in my heart. I began to weep and weep over these negative thoughts. How could I have deceived myself, thinking I was a loving person? I asked the Lord to forgive me, to cleanse me, to change me, and to root out this critical spirit, and then He told me what I must do. I was to take each name, and to actively remember the things that I had thought, the judgements I had made, and then to speak out words of release, such as "I release you from every judgement I have made, and where I've hurt you, I'm sorry, and I will ask your forgiveness when I am able." I did this over many days, knowing it was only the tip of the iceberg. The list only contained the names of people I worked with on a daily basis. I also testified in the fellowship to the way God was dealing with me and asked forgiveness both from God and from the individuals to whom God directed me personally. There was no place for self-consciousness or pride, I knew I was wrong, that this behaviour was not pleasing to God, and that He was in the process of radical and necessary heart surgery. At one point I became overwhelmed with my sin, and cried out to God saying, "I can never remember every thought or action, so how can I be forgiven?" He showed me a clear picture of a cooking tin. Most families have such a meat tin, and after much usage, the tin can look dirty, and yet be clean in the sense that it is grease-free. During dishwashing it may be proffered for inspection with words such as "Do you think I can get it cleaner than this?" and be answered, "No, it's been like that for years." In a similar way the Lord directed me to deal with the immediate, and He would take care of the past ingrained stains. This continued for many weeks. Suddenly a name or a face would come into my mind, and I would know I was being given another opportunity to release, and to be released.

God also showed me that my judgement was like a small snowball, which from insignificant beginnings gathers more and more snow and eventually becomes an enormous ball. I saw that my small judgements had grown into a huge weight of judgement, which is very dangerous if it should roll back on me. I looked up the many scriptures relating to judgement which I had been blind to. I had read them, but never applied them to myself.

Romans 14:4 says,

"Who are you to judge someone else's servant? To his own master he stands or falls. And he will stand, for the Lord is able to make him stand."

James 2:13 says,

"Judgement without mercy will be shown to anyone who has not been merciful. Mercy triumphs over judgement!"

And Jesus' own words in Matthew 7:1 are,

"Do not judge, or you too will be judged. For in the same way you judge others, you will be judged, and with the measure you use, it will be measured to you."

I saw plenty of specks of dust and inadequacies in others, but had failed to take the plank out of my own eye or heart. The more I repented, the more I saw positive rather than negative things in those I had formerly judged so harshly. I felt light and clean and joyful. I didn't stop seeing, but I no longer judged, rather compassion and love caused me to cry out for help when I saw it was needed.

Leaders often have their critical faculties enhanced, as they train themselves to be acutely aware of others, because of the responsibility they carry. In me it had become distorted in that I saw negatives, rather than positives; this was not Jesus' way of thinking. He saw what was in men's hearts, but he always saw how they could change; He judged no one. He gave many a way of escape. His love allowed people to change, and I began to see love working in me in a new way. The Holy Spirit is the Spirit of discernment, and He will often warn us, and show us areas of concern or even sin in others, but not so we make judgements, but rather that we can act with wisdom and grace.

As the Lord was dealing with these things in my heart, a new couple came to join the fellowship. They were popular, fun, and integrated well, but because of this root of judgement, they could do no right in my eyes. I found I had a very negative reaction to them, even though I had little contact at a personal level. If I saw them together in a supermarket, I judged him to be lazy, 'he should be working, not shopping.' I would smile and greet them, but inside, because of the numerous judgements I made, I was distancing myself from them, and yet they were a part of my Christian family, not my enemies. At one time they were involved in a minor car accident, and I judged them 'bad drivers', rather than showing kindness or compassion. The moment I dealt with the bitter root, which was secretly poisoning my relationship with them, everything changed. It was as if they became different people. I saw how they cared for each other, and for others. How they served joyfully, in all sorts of thankless tasks. They had not changed, I had, and with the plank removed from my eyes, love flowed. I do not claim perfection, but from the time of God's dealing with me, I have sought to positively release anyone I found myself judging. The result is that I am more compassionate and accepting, wanting the best for others, and I constantly remind myself, that if I point one finger at anyone, at least three others point back at me.

I now find that I am super sensitive to criticism, I wince when I hear negative remarks and will often challenge people and ask, "Will you now say something positive?" We so often do the devil's work for him with words that diminish other people. If you cannot say something positive, it is better to say nothing at all!

Jesus says,

"For out of the overflow of the heart the mouth speaks." (Matthew 12:34)

If your words and thoughts are critical then maybe your heart is in need of surgery. Listen to yourself. Do you use your tongue to build up or to tear down? To honour or to dishonour?

My father-in-law grew up in a Christian home, where sadly he suffered a great deal of personal criticism. As an adult he made a covenant with God to eradicate criticism from his tongue and to seek always to build others up by refusing to indulge negative speech. He trained himself to counter any negative comment with a positive, affirming statement. If you were the one speaking critically, you felt chastened, not judged. You simply wished you hadn't made such a foolish remark, and it put a halt to any ongoing, unhelpful conversation. Also, the absence of a critical spirit drew people to him and many received help, both spiritually and practically.

People instinctively know whether it is safe to share their intimate needs with someone else. Hurting humanity needs mercy not judgement.

Galatians 5:14-15 says

"Love you neighbour as yourself. If you keep on biting and devouring each other, watch out or you will be destroyed by each other."

For years I had prayed for more love for people, knowing my own shortfall. When I asked God to change me, He dealt with my hard heart and sensitised it so that I felt His sadness. Once my judgemental attitudes were exposed and rooted out, love flowed, relationships blossomed and people who had once avoided me sensed the difference and drew closer.

Jesus had compassion for the people to whom He ministered, He saw them as lost helpless sheep and reached out to help and rescue them. Jesus declared that He had come to seek and to save the lost, not to judge. I have had the privilege of ministering God's grace to a number of completely broken men and women. People who saw themselves as beyond redemption and could not believe that God was offering them mercy, not judgement. If there had been the slightest hint of judgement in me, I doubt if I could have been able to reach out to them. I am so thankful to the Holy Spirit for exposing this root and giving me the tools to see it removed. It is my responsibility to guard my heart in case old ways of reacting seek to once again rear their ugly heads.

Make it Personal

1   Ask the Holy Spirit to search your heart and see if you have any judgemental attitudes towards anyone.

2   Gaze at Jesus and meditate on his ability to show mercy.
    Read how Jesus treated the woman caught in the act of adultery – John 8:1-11

3   I needed God's mercy and grace to see the root of judgement dug out. It was a painful process but life transforming - Hebrews 4:16 says,

    "Let us then approach the throne of grace with confidence, so that we may receive mercy and find grace to help us in our time of need."

    He can help you to deal with this issue in your life.

Chapter 9

Healing old Wounds

Have you ever had a small thorn in your finger without realising it? The surface skin heals over, but each time you put pressure on a certain spot it hurts and lets you know there is something under the skin. On further investigation, you find the thorn and wonder that a small thing could cause such pain. Life's experiences cause wounds. Many times we forget the circumstances, but as with the thorn, when pressure is applied to that spot, we experience pain.

My son, Daniel borrowed my car; he tied the family 'Topper' on the roof rack and set off with his friends for an evening sailing off the south coast. The following morning the boat was still in place when I needed to take Ben to school. I set off and was not pleased to find the petrol gauge registering empty, but figured I had probably got enough fuel to get me to school and back. I knew I needed to address the issue of responsibility with Daniel and my mind was occupied with ways to approach this without causing strife. Suddenly a bus rounded a sharp corner taking all of my side of the road, I stood hard on the brake pedal, and as I did, to my horror the boat slid forward, bounced off the bonnet and onto the road. I was already irritated, now embarrassment and shock were added to the cocktail of emotions. Ben was sent back home to get Charles and Daniel and I stood at the roadside pretty steamed up! Rather than deal with the necessary corrections in a private and controlled manner, I hurled angry words at Daniel, which he countered, declaring that the fault lay in my driving rather than his failure to secure the boat adequately! I am not sure whether I drove to school on petrol or anger fumes, however, on returning home I needed to talk. Daniel expressed the opinion, that having driven 30 miles with the boat on the roof without incident, he was not to blame. I defended my driving and we reached an impasse with both of us extremely upset. Charles, whom I expected to defend me, listened to the argument without taking sides, and I was furious with him, but didn't understand why!

I struggled with forgiveness, I wanted someone to blame, feeling I was innocent. During the next few days, I went through the motions of forgiveness, but I kept rehearsing the issues in my mind and could not find a place of peace and closure. It was into this situation that God spoke to me and said, "Whenever you have an emotional reaction that is out of proportion to the incident that has caused it – you need healing." I cried out from my heart, "What needs healing? What is causing this pain and irrational behaviour?" Immediately I recalled an incident from my childhood. I had been accused of breaking a very precious piece of my mother's china, which I had not touched. My mother knew that I was not given to telling lies, but chose to believe the adult who had accused me and who had in fact been the culprit. She failed both to believe me and support me in the way I expected. Although I was only eight years old at the time, I was incensed with the injustice and punishment I received. I had been wounded but had no ability to process my feelings, and in time forgot – but the thorn was still embedded in my heart.

Thirty years later, I was in a new situation feeling unjustly accused, not believed and unsupported; the pain was intense. The difference now lay in my understanding of what was happening, now knowing how to extend forgiveness and let healing flow. I was led by the Holy Spirit to forgive the people involved in the earlier situation, and as I was praying, amazingly, Daniel came into the room to ask forgiveness for his part in the scenario, now fully acknowledging and taking responsibility for his actions. Once the old thorn was removed, it was easy to resolve this present situation.

I am not given to naval gazing and do not encourage people to focus on the past, unless the Holy Spirit shines His spotlight on a particular issue that needs His touch. However, when He does, I am fully confident He will heal what He exposes. Having trained myself, I have also trained my children to deal with any issues of forgiveness before they go to sleep, "Do not let the sun go down while you are still angry," (Ephesians 4:26) has been a principle in our home. I have discovered that if I disobey this instruction the problem doubles or trebles in size overnight, making it so much harder to handle. Human beings regularly wound each other, sometimes deliberately, but more often through carelessness, insensitivity and selfishness. I have been hurt, betrayed and misunderstood on many occasions; however, knowing my emotional health to be commensurate with my willingness to forgive, I've consistently worked through these issues to a place of forgiveness.

I became aware of another pattern of behaviour that I knew was wrong, where I could say "Yes!" to forgiveness, but "No!" to further trust. The Holy Spirit did not want me to harden or protect my heart, and so set out to "corner me." A very close friend, who I loved dearly and whose friendship I valued began to act strangely towards me. My first reaction was to think I'd imagined something that wasn't there, but over time, I instinctively knew something was wrong. Several times I questioned this friend. How had I offended? Had I failed in some way? I couldn't get to the bottom of it. I prayed for light to shine into the situation, as I watched our relationship deteriorate. Then one day I was presented with a list of offences big and small that I had committed over a period of five or six years. They had been building up steadily and now were dumped on me in a way that was overwhelming. I was totally unaware that my actions had caused such pain, and many of the accusations were half-truths and misunderstandings. We eventually talked openly and honestly, and were able to give and receive forgiveness, but we had bruised each other, however, as I still was in regular contact with this friend, I reacted by becoming extremely self protective, bending over backwards to make sure I didn't cause any further offence and in the process our relationship lost its spontaneity and became wooden and superficial. I did not want this, and neither did the Holy Spirit. It felt as if I was constantly walking on egg shells, could no longer open my heart for fear of being attacked, and was totally unable to trust or see the friendship develop any further.

One day I received a message asking me to make contact with this friend, as something needed to be talked through. Fearing I had done something else to offend, I allowed panic to grip my heart. I still had old wounds, even though I had forgiven and my heart started to throb, despite having tried to put self protecting barriers of indifference in place. I felt intimidated and remembered the word spoken to me once before, that if I was over-reacting it pointed to my need for healing. The phone call was to take place the following day and I couldn't sleep, my mind was racing, memories of the past confrontation rose up. I was planning what I would say and my emotions were raw. Finally I cried out to the One who is The Truth, and who always deals with His children kindly and justly for our ultimate good. Again, He showed me a childhood incident. A dog I adored had become sick, and I was told the dog had died. I knew it had an enlarged belly button and money for vet's bills was beyond the means of our family. I grieved but accepted the inevitable. In reality, but unbeknown to me, the dog was still alive and had been given to a family who lived some distance away and had the resources to care for it. Some time later I saw my dog, recognised the physical defect, and realised the dog was still alive. I was dreadfully upset and angry with all those who were involved with the deception, and at that time made a vow, "If you hurt me or let me down, I'll never trust you again." Something took hold of my young heart at that time and had started a pattern of behaviour. I liked people and expected the best of them, but once they had let me down, something shut down in the whole area of trust. It became relatively easy to keep relationships superficial and pleasant, but not open hearted or real. Now the Holy Spirit challenged this, He made me aware of what I was doing. He told me, in order to be able to trust again, I needed to forgive those who deceived me regarding the dog and allow Him to take the long buried pain, soften my heart and remove the self protective covering. Straight away I put my hand in the air and prayed for a complete healing and received it. In the morning I phoned my friend who only wanted to tell me some good news, but then I was able to explain all that had taken place during the night. The deep connection we once had was instantly restored and all fear left me. The Holy Spirit had also been at work in my friend, she was able to explain how she had listened to lies and misinterpreted my actions and allowed the devil's strategy to spoil our friendship.

Today that relationship is healthy, we fellowship when we are together, and both of us have experienced the healing that only Jesus can give. I have chosen to keep trusting, knowing I might experience further hurt. I'm aware that human beings are just that – human, only Jesus is totally trust worthy. Living, loving relationships are vital, we need each other and must make every effort to live at peace with all people, especially our fellow believers.

Make it Personal

1 Take a few minutes to reflect on any painful or broken relationships. Ask the Holy Spirit to expose any thorns – and let Him remove them.

2 Read the story of the Good Samaritan (Luke 10:25-37) Are there wounds that need cleansing and binding up? You might find it beneficial to pray things through with a trusted friend.

Chapter 10

Condemnation

To a greater or lesser degree, living under condemnation was a persistent feature of my early years as a Christian. In my head I understood that God loved me, and that when I sinned, and confessed, He would forgive me. However, in my heart I questioned this because I had failed Him so often. I was at this time quick-tempered, outspoken, and under stress I regularly lost all self-control, and gave vent to my anger. After I had 'exploded', I would be overcome with remorse, self-hatred, and condemnation. This pattern of behaviour was in itself unpleasant, but it was magnified by the contrast of that of my husband and his family, who had been trained in self-control. If they were upset or angry, their normal response would more likely be silence and withdrawal. The enemy had a field day, tormenting me both mentally and emotionally, telling me so many lies and half-truths, which I often believed. Thus a pattern emerged which kept me in a prison of condemnation. I would be living my normal life and some petty incident would happen that caused me to respond in anger. I would become verbally aggressive, I would shout at the offender, and generally behave in an out of control way. I was always quick to repent, and to ask for forgiveness from whoever had incurred my 'wrath', but I hated what I did, and especially what I said. I knew it was wrong and harmful, I would seek and receive God's forgiveness, but found it almost impossible to forgive myself. A pattern emerged, which would begin with an incident, was followed by a verbal explosion, then by sadness, guilt, and shame, and as the memory faded, I would gradually reconnect with God until the next time. It was destructive and exhausting, but I could not break the cycle. I sought God for more self-control; I tried so hard to button my mouth, and push down the emotions, but to no avail. Knowing self-control to be a fruit of the Holy Spirit, and being so aware of its absence in my life, I began to question how I could possibly be filled with God's Holy Spirit.

Life at this time was demanding. We had three small children, a large house, part of which was used for our youth club, which meant that there was a constant flow of the young people filling the house after school and at weekends. We also had a young lady living with us, who was recovering from a mental breakdown. I can see now that I was stretched to capacity, which served to expose this area of weakness that might possibly have remained hidden given a different set of circumstances. One particular Thursday, which was Charles' half-day, we took the children to the north of Cornwall, to look at and possibly purchase some granite gateposts for our garden. Small children in the car for any length of time are not usually peaceful and content, and this journey proved no exception. We arrived home to find that our young lodger had unsuccessfully attempted some baking, and then taken to her bed - leaving my kitchen in the most appalling mess! I was expecting Don Double for a meal in less than two hours, and my reaction was predictable and very unpleasant. I released my tension by shouting at everybody, which didn't help; and finally, when order was restored, forgiveness given and received, the children fed and put to bed, we welcomed Don as if nothing had happened.

I have no recollection of how I cooked that meal nor of what it consisted, but I do remember the ensuing conversation in detail. Charles and Don began to discuss whether or not it was possible to live without sin. They were enjoying themselves as they explored the theology surrounding this question. I was irritated, never liking theoretical questions, and I could feel anger rising in me. I was still raw from the earlier incident, but was also trying to be on my best behaviour. We considered it an honour to have Don in our home. Eventually, unable to remain silent, I declared that no one could live without sinning, and that I certainly sinned constantly. I then recounted the events, which had taken place only a few hours earlier. Don listened with great patience to my tale of woe, as by now my tears were flowing freely, and it was obvious that I needed help to resolve what was a recurring problem.

Don began by asking several questions, to which I gave answers, and this led him to tell me a parable in the form of a drama. He was quick to realise that I had no practical understanding of God's grace. In theory, I knew that if I confessed, and renounced my sin, I would be forgiven. But being forgiven and feeling that I was forgiven, were two totally different concepts.

Don began the drama with a typical incident set in our house.

Scene 1:

Something trivial would start me off on a chain of events resulting in an explosion of angry words.

All of this was being observed by satan, who also fuelled the fire, and the scenario ended with me being totally out of control.

Scene 2:

This next scene was similar to the beginning chapters of the book of Job, where satan appears before God, not this time to accuse Job, but to accuse Joyce.

He was rehearsing all my failure and sin in detail before the Almighty.

God, who after verifying the name, looked up 'Sibthorpe' in His record books, while satan peered over His shoulder, eager to see a record of this angry behaviour it all its gory detail, but to his horror there was nothing recorded.

The page was clean, blank, save for two scriptures written in red.

1 John 1:9:
If we confess our sins, he is faithful and just and will forgive us our sins and purify us from all unrighteousness.

1 John 1:7:
The blood of Jesus Christ, God's Son, cleanses us from all sin.

Satan tried to argue that this could not be, but was dismissed.

Scene 3:

I'm feeling battered and sore, I have confessed my sin, and understood that by doing so, I am forgiven, but I have failed to forgive myself, and consequently, I am in torment.

Satan capitalising on my raw emotions and self-hatred, is quick to lie to me. He appears sitting near me, whispering words of condemnation in my ear. Words that I had heard many times before, "How can you call yourself a Christian? You don't act like one. You fail so often. God will get fed up of forgiving you. You really are a bad mother, aren't you? Your children will grow up and reject you. All they will remember of their childhood is their mother shouting at them."

These were familiar words, and before Don finished telling the final part of his small drama, I could see clearly how I had been tricked into believing the enemy's lies. I had not understood God's provision of instant forgiveness and cleansing, and I had lived under a cloud of condemnation, from which I emerged only to fail again and again. Don explained to me how satan operates, and how Jesus dealt with him, when He Himself was tempted. He reminded me that Jesus used the Word of God saying, "It is written", and then quoted scripture, which dismissed the devil, who unable to oppose the Word, had to leave. Don encouraged me, then and there, to rebuke satan, and to tell him to go, using scripture in the way that he had just described. Feeling extremely foolish and vulnerable, but desperate to find a way of escape from the prison of condemnation, I told the devil, "It is written ....", and then with growing confidence, on Don's instructions, I rebuked him, using the Name of Jesus, and finally I forgave myself, and began to thank God for His amazing grace and provision. That night I walked out of a prison. My chains fell off, and I knew that I had the tools to fight and win. It took time, but I knew increasing victory. And when I failed, I quietly confessed and remembered the page in the heavenly ledger, which was blank. Later I learned, instead of pleading with God for more self-control, to choose rather to keep seeking to be so filled with the Holy Spirit that the fruit of the Holy Spirit - self-control - could grow bigger and stronger.

During World War II, a young RAF bomber pilot discovered a rat in the fuselage of his 'plane. Fearing it might somehow detonate the bombs he was carrying, he radioed to headquarters for instructions. He and his crew were told to immediately put on oxygen masks, and to ascend to a higher altitude. As the aircraft climbed higher, the oxygen in the air became inadequate, and very soon the rat was dead. The pilot, relying on his oxygen supply, was sustained in the rarefied atmosphere, and flew on to finish his mission. In a similar way, as I breathe in the life of the Holy Spirit, I will live, and the 'rat of my flesh' will be starved to death.

In the Old Testament, sinners were required to bring a perfect lamb without spot or blemish as an offering. First it was presented to the priest for his inspection, and if it passed the test, it was then sacrificed. Who did the priest inspect for faults and blemishes? Was it the sinner who brought the offering or the lamb that would become the sacrifice? Obviously it was the lamb. The lamb was perfect and took the place of the sinner, who deserved death. The sinner was forgiven, cleansed, and allowed to go free. All this was looking forward to Jesus, 'the Lamb of God', who takes away the sin of the world. The sinner was trusting in the sacrifice of a perfect lamb. Our Jesus was, is, and will forever be, sinless and perfect, and His sacrifice has been accepted, and is eternally effective. I remain capable of sinning, and in need of forgiveness, but I no longer inspect myself, but rather choose to trust in the fact that God has accepted Jesus as my sacrifice. As the hymn says,

"In my place condemned He stood,
sealed my pardon with His blood,
Hallelujah, what a Saviour!"

This truth has been life changing for me, and it has always been a great joy for me to share it with others. At one time, I was asked to pray for a young woman who desperately needed to know she could receive God's forgiveness, peace and healing. The story was very sad. She had given birth to a child that looked perfect, but whose heart was defective, and the baby died in her arms, shortly after birth. However, before the baby had been conceived, this young woman had been tempted to enter into an extra-marital affair. She had resisted, and taken steps to remove herself from the situation of temptation. Her husband had been fully aware of what happened, had forgiven her, and together they had succeeded in strengthening their marriage.

They had been overjoyed to discover the pregnancy, but when the baby died, satan started to bring his vile accusations. In her grief and weakness, this young woman believed she had been responsible for the death of her child, and that she was being punished by God. The mental accusations were endless and eventually led to her having a emotional breakdown. She slowly recovered and was being restored with the help and support of a loving husband, friends, and family. However, her relationship with God was distant, and she was still carrying a lot of guilt and much confusion. She came to see me, having discovered she was again pregnant, and was full of fear in case her earlier experience would be repeated. I used Don's drama, applying it to her circumstances, and suddenly she saw how she had been deceived. Her self-condemnation had led to the breakdown. And that night, as we prayed, she was held in God's loving arms, and restored. Subsequently, she gave birth to a beautiful boy, and went on to have several other children. This song wonderfully expresses these truths:

"I am a new creation, no more in condemnation,
Here in the grace of God I stand.
My heart is overflowing, my love just keeps on growing.
Here in the grace of God I stand.
And I will praise you Lord, and I will praise you Lord.
And I will sing of all that you have done."

That is a modern song, but expresses the same truths as in Wesley's wonderful old hymn:

"No condemnation now I dread;
Jesus, and all in Him, is mine.
Alive in Him, my living Head,
and clothed in righteousness Divine.
My chains fell off, my heart was free.
I rose, went forth and followed Thee."

It amazes me how many people who love Jesus, who have been Christians for many years, have failed to grasp this truth. One morning, I was asked if I would visit the prison in Horfield, Bristol. A young man, known to our family, was in custody having just killed his wife. The circumstances were tragic. While he had been working away from home, his wife had been involved in an affair. He had returned unexpectedly to their home, and discovered the evidence in photographs which lay around the house. His wife was out at the time, but when she returned he had confronted her, and in his white-hot anger had shaken her to death. There was no question about his guilt, which he admitted and he had even tried to take his own life. I went to Horfield Prison, and as I sat outside in the car, wondered what on earth I could say. God gave me a word for this young man, which I wrote on the back of an envelope. What He said was very simple. I was told me to tell him that if he would confess his sin, and ask for forgiveness, even this awful crime could be blotted out from God's sight. In the sight of the law he had to face trial and punishment, but in God's sight he could be cleansed, because Jesus had taken the full weight of that sin in His own body at Calvary. The young man, although in a dreadful state, was able to receive that word, which subsequently brought him into a place of forgiveness and peace, and a place where he understood how great the grace of God is. He deserved death, but instead he got life. There are believers who have no understanding of the depth of God's forgiveness, and even to this day, cannot understand how someone like this can live a life free from guilt and condemnation. Jesus said that it is those who have been forgiven much who love much, and the love that he received is now expressed by this man in prison ministry, where he can go to some of the most hardened criminals in this land, and tell them that there is a way out. As the words of an old chorus say,

"There's a way back to God from the dark path of sin;
There's a door that is open and you may go in.

At Calvary's cross is where we begin,
When you come as a sinner to Jesus."

Make it Personal

1 How do you see yourself? As a sinner trying to keep clean or a righteous man or woman?

2 Consider the sinless Lamb of God. He is the perfect, spotless Lamb who stood in your place. He was inspected, accepted and slaughtered – all your sin, guilt and shame were laid on him. He became your substitute and you go free – forgiven.

3 Give thanks that you are accepted in Jesus.
Read Exodus 12:1-42
Read John 1: 29-34
Read Hebrews 10:13-18   One sacrifice – for sin – for ever.

4 Psalm 130:3-4 says, *"If you, O Lord kept a record of sins, who could stand BUT with you there is forgiveness therefore you are to be feared."*

5 Declare yourself to be righteous because of the sacrifice Jesus made.

Chapter 11

Rest

In 1984, God began to speak to me about living from a place of rest. At the time my life was extremely busy, with a household of five children, aged between eight and eighteen, my elderly father and three single people. Each had their own needs, the children were in various stages of growth, my father was in failing health, and the single folk, one of whom was a recovering drug addict, all had considerable needs. Into this situation God began to talk about rest. I have been in the habit of writing a daily journal and here are some of the things God was saying to me at that time:

1st October 1984: Rest in me and let me fill your heart anew with my love, with joy and excitement at my presence. I want you to experience again the tenderness and nearness of my presence. I want you to fall in love with me again, to worship and rejoice that I love you, and have called you; that I provide and direct you. I want to release your heart to be thrilled with me and as a result to worship.

11th October 1984: Rest in me. Release your father to me. Do not be afraid. His life is in my hands.

12th October 1984: Rest in the Lord, wait patiently for Him, and He will give you your heart's desire. I want to speak to you about rest. It is not an absence of work or pressure, or demand, but it is an inner assurance that I am in control. It involves faith, because what you see and hear with your senses is not what is actually happening, and you must learn to exercise faith in order to be able to rest, and trust me to work.

29th October 1984: You asked me about Sundays. Firstly, I declare Sunday to be a day of rest, not a day to do nothing, but a day to do different things. Make it a unique day, let it be a day to look forward to, perhaps you could eat in the evening or let the children cook. I would like you to celebrate the Sabbath and bless other people. I want it to be a rejoicing day, but also a day of giving you time to think. Make it a delight, something everyone will enjoy and look forward to. You can go out; you do not need to be bound to the house. I release you to experiment. Sunday is a gift to you. A day to enjoy, free from work, and a day when I used to say "rest", but you will understand it better when I say "relax". Planning and preparation are essential, and must be done during the week.

24th April 1985: Rest is the quality I want to place deep within your soul, a rest and peace that nothing and no one can disturb. I want you to live life to the full but always from a place of peace and deep rest. This is reality, a rock-like quality which is solid, and dependable. Where there is rest there will be also be joy; joy lightens each day, and each contact. Rest is heart relationship where you are deeply rooted into me, and drawing from my resources; being refreshed even as you live life. You have been seeking rest through order and planning, but the rest I am speaking of comes from relationship, trust and obedience.

7th June 1985: I want you to live in me today, consciously acknowledging my presence, and enjoying me. I am in you and you're in me. Rest in me today, and I will bless you.

27th November 1985: Do you not think that there are times when I call you to relax, to rest, and simply do nothing? I want you to enjoy living.

22nd January 1986: Enjoy what I give you to do. Rest in me today; I long to see you with a rest of spirit, and with joy.

I have always loved Psalm 131, which speaks of God's people being like a weaned child in its mother's arms. If you have ever watched a baby sated with milk, asleep, and totally relaxed, it is a wonderful picture of rest. Imagine yourself trustfully held by your loving Father, who is more than able to care for you and meet all your needs. There have been times when I have known such rest, but then resorted to living by my own self-effort, losing that rest and consequently experiencing not only a loss of joy, but also of strength. Sometimes I would quickly realise what was happening and run back to Jesus, but at other times I would stubbornly press on, until my own resources had completely run out. Only then would I see the futility of self-effort and repent. Our Father God is so patient when He wants to teach us a lesson; He will keep talking about the subject until we get it. He doesn't seem to mind how long it takes; but will gently brings us back to basics and reinforce the thing that He wants to teach us. I had the wrong idea that rest was a place that I would arrive at when there were no crises, no demands being made of me, and when I had achieved order in the external circumstances of my life. I never got there; in fact, I wonder if such a place exists, apart from in my imagination.

So often the Holy Spirit would tell me, "Rest is an inner place of connection with Jesus. Rest is a relationship of trust. It is leaning on the One who is in control, who knows every detail of my life, and who has resources and strategies for every emergency." God's training programme is for our good, it is not to punish us, but rather to release us into heavenly resources. It is to live in a heavenly dimension, which takes us out of the ordinary into the extraordinary, and from the natural into the supernatural. His goal for us is abundant living.

One day, when I certainly was not in a place of rest, I began to complain to God about the pressure and the difficulties I was experiencing, and crying out for Him to help me. At the time I was reading the New Testament in the Message, and I came across Matthew 11:28-29,

> *"Are you tired? Worn out? Burned out on religion? Come to me. Get away with me and you will recover your life. I'll show you how to take a real rest. Walk with me and work with me – watch how I do it. Learn the unforced rhythms of grace. I won't lay anything heavy or ill fitting on you. Keep company with me, and you'll learn to live freely and lightly."*

It was as if a bolt of lightning had hit me, and in an instant I saw my foolishness and lack. This is how I wanted to live, but more importantly, this is how God wanted me to live, and He had been trying to show me that. However, every time He spoke to me about rest, I had failed to get the message. Each truth that really impacts our lives comes with revelation, and this was no exception.

Hebrews 4:11 says,

> *"Let us, therefore, make every effort to enter that rest."*

Making every effort seems a contradiction in terms, but when you realise what you have been offered, you are eager to embrace this quality of life. And so I asked the Lord to allow me to enter His rest, and willingly began to co-operate and seek His help to enter and to stay there. Occasionally now, I hear the Lord rebuke me with such words as, "You have been chasing your tail again, wasting energy, and not recharging your batteries. Even as you read my Word you are rushing to finish it, so that you can do something else. This is not how I want you to live." Once we set our hearts to obey, the Holy Spirit will come alongside and help us.

It was during this time that one night I awoke at about 3am, and after failing to get back to sleep, decided to get out of bed and spend some time with the Lord. A verse of scripture was rolling around in my head, "Be still, and know that I am God", so I decided to look it up and see the context. I was using an NIV Study Bible at the time, and my eyes were drawn to the notes which said this, "Be still" - the Hebrew means 'enough' as in 'stop', and acknowledge that "I am God." As I read, the presence of the Lord became really strong, and I found myself weeping, aware that this was no ordinary moment, God was deeply challenging me. My response to Him was, "I don't know how to be still, nor how to rest. I want to live out of your resources, but I acknowledge my wilfulness and how I leave the place of stillness and rest without even realising." The Lord's gracious word to me was, "I will teach you - Be still – you know very little about stillness, rest, waiting, abiding, quietness, but I will teach you by demonstrating the value of being with me, no agenda, just being together. We don't even need to talk. I can understand you without words, and so can you understand me. Let's practise." That night I simply sat in my kitchen, and took time to be still. I had to deliberately dismiss the demands of the coming day. People's needs would invade my mind and then I would realise I was not still. And so began a season of waking each morning at about 3am, and of being taught to simply 'be' in the presence of the Lord. It got to a point that I couldn't wait to wake up. The house was quiet, the traffic outside was at a minimum, and there I would sit, still, until I felt the Lord dismiss me, and send me back to bed. I might get an hour's sleep; the length of time was irrelevant. I was completely energised, not by the hours of unconsciousness, but by the life-giving presence of Jesus. Several scriptures became real and personal during that season.

Psalm 37:7,

"Be still before the Lord and wait patiently for him."

Exodus 14:14:

"The Lord will fight for you; you need only to be still."

Exodus 33:14,

"My presence will go with you, and I will give you rest."

I saw how much the Lord wants us to function out of His resources and not our own.

Isaiah 28:12 made me so sad,

"This is the resting-place, let the weary rest; and "This is the place of repose," - but they would not listen." And verse 13 says, "So then, the Word of the Lord to them will become: Do and do, do and do, rule on rule, rule on rule; here a little, there a little – so that they will go and fall backward, be injured and snared and captured."

Isaiah 30:15,

"In repentance and rest is your salvation, in quietness and trust is your strength, but you would have none of it."

The more I live in rest, the less I enjoy chasing my tail. Like David, I quickly find myself speaking to my own soul the psalmist's words.

Psalm 116:7,

"Be at rest once more, O my soul."

It's not easy to recount the Lord's dealings with me during those times as most of it was silent communication, but the effect of living from this new place of stillness and rest has had immense benefits. It was as if I had supernatural strength, which indeed, I did have. Tiredness wasn't a word in my vocabulary when I was living from this source. As long as I was still, I had everything I needed.

During this time I was asked to take a Ladies' Day Conference in Sussex. The Lord had given me the word, and I was excited to see what He would do. I had a three-hour car journey from my home, so an early start was necessary, and therefore, logically, I needed a reasonably early night. But I could not sleep. I tried every thing; I rebuked sleeplessness, I prayed for sleep; I even woke my husband to pray, but still no sleep. Then Jesus spoke, "Be still, lie in my arms and rest." I watched the hours tick by, awake, but at peace. At 5am, I started the day, drove 300 miles, taught throughout the day, returned home and went to bed at the normal time, still full of energy and strength. It was not natural; strength came from the source of intimate contact with the One who is a life-giving Spirit. Not only was I amazed at what had happened, but this incident released me completely from fear of sleep deprivation. The physical resources we need come from the Lord, not simply from the hours we lie horizontal. I look back at this time as "a beginning of days," a completely new way of living, and a new revelation. This is how Jesus lived, never pushing people away, never being self-protective. He had intimate contact with the Father from whom flowed all that He needed. He spent nights alone with God, while the disciples slept. Whenever He had spent the entire day meeting the needs of others, He would retreat to fellowship with his Father and His batteries would be recharged. He understood the need to find quiet places to relax, but when His attempts were thwarted, He wasn't frustrated, but rather pushed deeper into the Father's resources.

Some of you may be thinking, "OK, you're talking about Jesus, but I'm human, so is it possible for me to live like this?" My answer is, "Yes". I've watched others do it and, in spite of my own limitations, I have proved that I can live out of divine connection, I can indeed do all things through Christ who strengthens me.

In December 2007, I returned home from a busy time of ministry in Nigeria to a very demanding schedule, and only five days before Christmas. The family were all gathering for my daughter's 40th birthday. Craig and Milena and their family from Bulgaria had already arrived at our house. Ben and Anne were back from Africa with their three young children, and a newborn baby, and we picked up Coralie and her baby Judson as we passed through London Heathrow. All our children were together for the first time in ten years to celebrate Joanna's birthday on 23rd December. It was as busy a time as we had ever known, but I was not stressed. I worked hard, I enjoyed serving, I had time one-on-one with family members, and the atmosphere was relaxed, which had the effect of releasing others to see what needed to be done, and doing it. My own children were quite amazed. Normally, with so many people around, and such a lot of work, I could be snappy, stressed, and demanding. But not this time, because I had changed my source of living. It was not human energy, but it came from divine contact, heavenly resources.

I have had the privilege of working alongside several well-known Christian leaders, and in doing so, have seen their strengths and weaknesses. In recent years, I have been privileged to be part of a ministry in Nigeria, called Living Seed. The leader of the team lives in the way I have described. His life-source comes from his connection with Jesus. In seven years I have never seen him ruffled, rude, or self-occupied. He is always gracious, alert, he has the main responsibility of teaching the 15,000 folk who attend a Retreat each year, and yet he has time to talk to individuals, and demonstrate a genuine interest in their lives. Often people will comment on his lack of self-protection, his ability to finish preaching, and then go straight into a planning session about a building development, or a printing press problem. How does he do it? He knows the secret of living out of rest, and stillness. In Hebrews 4:10 it says, "...anyone who enters into God's rest also rests from his own work." We are encouraged to make every effort to enter that rest, to abide in Jesus, and to do no uncommanded work, but only as instructed by Him. This is the most joyful way to live and work. The more we experience this joy, the more strength will be available, and we will have entered a life-giving cycle: I come to Jesus, I rest in Him, I'm enlivened, I live, I enjoy what I am commanded to do, and with a heart full of thanksgiving and praise I return to the source of life, and repeat the cycle.

Make it Personal

1   Listen to this well-known hymn – paste this link into your internet browser
    http://www.cyberhymnal.org/htm/i/h/iheardtv.htm
    I heard the voice of Jesus say, "Come unto Me and rest;
    Lay down, thou weary one, lay down Thy head upon My breast."
    I came to Jesus as I was, weary and worn and sad;
    I found in Him a resting place, and He has made me glad.
                                        Written by Horatius Bonar (1846)

2   Come to Jesus, and imagine leaning your whole weight on Him. He can scan your heart, mind, and body. Let Him take your weariness.
    1 Peter 5:7 says,
      "Cast all your cares upon Him for He cares for you."

Hebrews 12:1-2 says,

"Let us throw off everything that hinders and the sin that so easily entangles....let us fix our eyes on Jesus the author and perfecter of our faith."

3 Listen to or download the short message entitled "The Motor Bike" on www.the222trust.org.uk

4 Read John 6:16-21 and see what happened when Jesus' disciples decided to go it alone. Look at their plight when they did that and what happened when Jesus came into the situation.

5 Hebrews 4:9-10 declares,
   "There remains, then, a Sabbath-rest for the people of God; for anyone who enters God's rest also rests from his own work, just as God did from his."

6 Our bodies are fuelled by the food we eat – once the energy released is used up, we need to refuel. Living from a place of rest can be likened to having an internal never-ending supply of every resource you will need. Jesus said, "I am the bread of life." Is He your life-source?

Chapter 12

The Death Principle

During a mission to the City of Manchester some years ago, Charles accompanied Colin Urquhart on a visit to Strangeways Prison where he had been invited to address the prisoners. Charles knew that only ten minutes had been allotted for the talk and wondered just how Colin would deal with the situation, as he normally spoke for at least an hour. Colin walked into the chapel packed with men, many of whom only used the chapel service as an excuse to be released from their cells. He greeted the men with these words, "I've got good news for you!" and a few of the men started cheering. He continued, "God doesn't want to reform you." The cheers grew louder, and when the noise had subsided, he said, "God wants you to die." A stunned silence fell on the gathered company, as Colin explained the truth of death and resurrection. In those ten minutes he explained clearly that if we identify with the death of Jesus, and see ourselves dying with Him on the cross, then we can also be raised to new life, not just a life of self-improvement, but a resurrection. We become brand-new and are empowered by God himself. The prisoners listened and some responded; they did not need reminding of the futility of trying to change themselves. Here was good news. A brand new start! A popular Christian song at that time had these words,

"I'm a new creation, I'm a brand new man.
Old things are passed away,
I've been born again.
More than a conqueror, that's who I am.
I'm a new creation, I'm a brand new man."

As this time we were living at The Hyde, and as a community we were learning to live out the truth and reality that if we had Christ in us, we were new men and women. We were not only learning how to change our thinking but also our words and actions. So if someone was faced with a task that in the past may have evoked an "I can't do that" response, we would encourage them to say and believe, "I can do all things through Christ who strengthens me." Knowing in our hearts that it was Christ at work, not our own human effort, we would be praying "You do it Lord. You're my wisdom. You have all knowledge." As we yielded to the Holy Spirit we rejoiced at His ability to enable us to achieve things that we had never dreamt possible. The reality of just 'Who' indwelt us was beginning to take effect; our outward appearance looked the same, but inwardly we were being changed on a daily basis.

Charles was teaching these truths of "Christ in you" in the south of Germany, and as part of his message he explained that when Christ lives in us, His whole personality and presence is alive within. He went on to say that as Jesus was never depressed, neither should we be, if we let Christ indwell us. This prompted a very strong reaction in a severely depressed lady who came for prayer. She insisted that she was a Christian, but argued that it was too simplistic, that it could never be that easy. Charles tried to explain to her that Jesus was anointed with joy and peace, and if He was allowed to live His life in her body, she could let the depression die, and begin to experience a totally new life. She was not prepared to receive this life transforming truth and went away unchanged.

This made Charles very sad, as he had recently seen this truth bring freedom to a severely depressed man who had phoned the Hyde and asked the question, "Do you do deliverance? I think I need to be delivered." Charles assured him that if he needed deliverance, we could do that, but suggested that they meet together. When Alan arrived his countenance and whole demeanour was that of a broken, sick man. His whole life story was heart breaking to listen to, and when asked about his experience of Christ, Alan proceeded to list all his church connections and religious activities. Charles was getting nowhere, when God prompted him to ask a question, "Alan, have you ever been to the cross?" "No" was the slightly stunned reply. Charles went on to explain that if Alan would bring all of his life, his disappointment, his sadness and despair, to the cross, Jesus would take these away and give him a brand new start. Charles explained that the cross is the place where Jesus died, but it is 'by faith' the place where I die, and when I die, I can also be resurrected, as a totally new man. He explained what it means to be born again and become a Christian: one in whom Christ dwells. That day Alan took himself, his brokenness, pain, sorrow, anger, failure, as well as his successes, his reputation - all that he was - and he willingly offered himself to be put to death with Jesus. There were many tears of relief as he let go of long-held burdens. And when he rose from his knees, he was indeed a brand new man. He had gone to death, and received life. It showed as his face was glowing, his demeanour changed, he looked years younger, and he never looked back. The change was permanent. He never spoke again about deliverance. He had experienced a new life lived with Jesus, and all trace of depression left him. Over the next few years we got to know Alan very well, and can testify to this complete healing.

God also brought to me a new understanding of the conversation Jesus had with Nicodemus. In John 3, when Nicodemus was finding it impossible to understand what it meant to be born again, Jesus reminded him of an incident recorded in Numbers 21 where it says that the children of Israel were yet again behaving rebelliously. As a consequence they had been bitten by snakes, and were dying in large numbers. Moses cried out to God, and God gave very specific instructions, "Make a replica snake in bronze and place it on a pole, and tell the people to look at it and they will live. Those who believed and looked, experienced life and healing. Those who thought it was too simple or stupid to believe that looking at the bronze replica snake could help them, didn't look, and didn't live! Jesus, speaking of Himself, said, "…so the Son of Man must be lifted up, that everyone who believes in Him may have eternal life." Notice the word "may." It seems to indicate choice, that if you believe, you will live. It is still a reality that people who look at the Son of Man, will by believing, receive this new eternal resurrected life.

Many people think that what I have described is simplistic, but I call it miraculous, and it can happen to all who see their need to look and live. Very recently a friend of mine attended a church in Bristol, and at the end of the service an invitation to receive Jesus was given. Several people came to the front of the church, and the pastor began to speak to them. He said, "The Christian life is about death to self. We all have to die to our own self-will, self-desires, and fleshly appetites. You can die slowly or quickly. I want to explain how to die quickly, and then you can understand how you can really live." My friend was moved, and amazed; also thrilled that this pastor was so straightforward. The Christian life is a life under new ownership, going in a new direction, with new thinking, new destiny, new everything. It is not trying to change the old self. Can you think of anything more revolting than carrying a dead body around with you, trying to stop it stinking?

Many Christians are concentrating on improving the old, and fail to realise or believe what Paul writes in Romans 6:6-7,

"For we know that our old self was crucified with him so that the body of sin might be done away with, that we should no longer be slaves to sin - because anyone who has died has been freed from sin. Now if we died with Christ, we believe that we will also live with him."

Baptism is the powerful symbol of death. I die as I am immersed into Christ, and I rise as I come out of the waters and into new life, often with a new name, and certainly with a new future.

Saul the religious, legalistic opponent of the early church met the living Jesus on the Damascus Road. He heard His voice, experienced blindness for three days, and when he received his sight, he was commissioned and filled with the Holy Spirit. Immediately he was baptised. Saul died, and a new man rose, Paul servant of the Most High God, totally changed, and so it should be for everyone who claims to be a Christian. The name means 'one in whom Christ lives.'

Paul's own words in Galatians 2:20 say this,

"I have been crucified with Christ and I no longer live, but Christ lives in me. The life I live in the body, I live by faith in the Son of God, who loved me and gave himself for me. I do not set aside the grace of God, for if righteousness could be gained through the law, then Christ died for nothing!"

After teaching on this theme in Manchester, I was approached by an older lady. She thanked me and then went on to say that if only she had understood these truths, she would have been saved from years of trouble. She had been trying to perfect something rotten, and hadn't succeeded, but she said, "Tonight I see that I have to die, and in doing so, I can forget my past, and can begin to live my new life." She had got it. Hallelujah!

Kenneth Hagin Sr. believed totally in the death principle. He used to tell how as a boy he had an amazing ability to pick locks. It was a natural talent, and the kids in his small town would encourage him to pick the lock on the village sweet shop. Once it was opened, they would help themselves. Kenneth always said that he would only open the door, and the others stole the sweets. Whether he ate them or not, I don't know, but he certainly was complicit. Years later, he visited his home town, and was recognised by one of the lads he used to hang around with, and they began to reminisce.

"Kenneth, remember how we used to break into the local shop?"
Kenneth's reply was, "That man is dead."
"Come on Kenneth, you used to pick the lock."
Kenneth, with deadpan expression on his face said, "That man's dead."

And to every recollection he gave the same answer. He so completely believed that he was a new creation that he could have this conversation with no embarrassment, and seemingly no explanation. He knew that the old Kenneth had indeed died and that he had been born again. He refused to live in the past, only in the present, and the future.

Make it Personal

1   In Acts 5:20 the angel of the Lord brought the apostles out of the public jail with these instructions,
     *"Go and stand in the temple courts and tell the people the full message of **this new life**."*

Paul's letters talk more fully about this, explaining the principle, whilst in the Acts of the Apostles we see a practical demonstration of this truth. See Romans 6:14, 2 Corinthians 5:17, Galatians 6:15, Colossians 3:9-10. Read these scriptures and ask the Holy Spirit to open your eyes.

2. Are you living the new life or are you still trying to improve the old?

3. Have you ever been to the cross in the way described in Alan's story? If not then make a new beginning today.

Chapter 13

Living Resurrection Life

"The best thing to do is to give yourself a decent burial, and get on with your new life. God's Spirit beckons. There are things to do, and places to go! This resurrection life you received from God is not a timid, grave-tending life. It's adventurously expectant, greeting God with a childlike, "What's next, Papa?" God's Spirit touches our spirits, and confirms who we really are."

That is how Romans 8:13-16 reads in The Message.

I used to think that God was working on me in much the same way as a sculptor on a block of stone. He was chipping away at the bits He didn't like, and remaking me into His original design. This left me with the feeling of inadequacy, and passivity, waiting for the day when I would be good enough to pass muster, and then I would become a John the Baptist or a Saul of Tarsus. The focus, when I think like that, is on me, my inadequacy, my performance, my ability, and it is totally contrary to New Testament teaching. Jesus said of Himself,

"For I did not speak of my own accord, but the Father who sent me commanded me what to say and how to say it." John 12:49

Nowadays I am seeking to be like a glove that God Himself puts on, and in which He moves his fingers as He chooses. The glove has no function without the hand filling it.

In the late 1890's a young woman, Amy Semple, was passing through London with her husband Robert, on their way to China. They were American missionaries, contemporaries of Hudson Taylor. Robert Semple was already a household name and was asked to speak at several large church gatherings. Amy was just eighteen years old and newly married, but she clearly understood Christ lived in her mortal body, and that she was a carrier of Jesus. When Robert was asked if his wife would speak to a gathering of ladies, he said that she would be delighted. She expected a small select group, but to her amazement Amy found herself addressing a large gathering of high-society ladies, eager both to hear Robert's new wife, and to support their mission work. It is reported that she gave an outstanding presentation of the book of Hosea, that she spoke with insight, and boldness, and that afterwards when she was being congratulated, she was quick to announce, "I know hardly anything about Hosea, the Holy Spirit was speaking, and I was simply His mouthpiece".

At one time I was asked to speak at the morning teaching meeting of Eagle Camp, which was a summer family camp where more than a thousand would spend a week in fellowship, teaching and fun. At the time it was the largest group of people before whom I had ever spoken. I knew of this challenge for many weeks, and spent much time seeking God for His word. He instructed me to read the book of Jonah, but gave me no idea of what He wanted to say. Each time I asked Him for a word, so that I could write an outline, I got nothing, except the instruction to carry on reading the book of Jonah. I continued doing this, but right up to the moment I stood up to speak, I had no clear indication of what to say. However, I knew the text, and the Holy Spirit applied the contents. I had never preached in this way before, and was amazed at the insight the Spirit of God brought out, and the emphasis he put on several verses. However, it was not me speaking, and I could not take the credit. Since then, there have been several occasions, on which I have had a scripture as a starting point, but I've had to trust the Lord for wherever He wants to go from there. At other times, I know clearly before I speak the main points that I am to address, but often the Holy Spirit will add his own touches and illustrations, and it is always these additions that have the most impact. I want to emphasise that this is not an excuse for laziness in preparation, or lack of seeking God to get a prepared word. Increasingly I seek to be a clear, sensitive channel that God's Spirit can use.

A friend of mine was asked to bring the keynote message at a very prestigious gathering of academic evangelicals. He was under pressure to perform. He set aside time to seek God for what he should bring, and during that time he felt God ask him a question,

"Why have you come here?"

His answer was, "To meet with you, and to receive the word for this particular gathering."

Another question followed, "Who did they invite, you or me?"

"You Lord", was his prompt reply."

"Then let me speak. You simply carry me there, and while you're here, let us fellowship together."

And so he spent days, just in company with the Lord. He eventually went to his convention, with no clear idea of what he should say, but at just the right moment the Holy Spirit began to expound 2 Corinthians Chapters 4, 5 and 6, and he found himself to be a mouthpiece, hearing revelatory truths out of his mouth, but for the first time. Why should it be a strange thing for the divine Author to explain what He wrote 2000 years ago? Does He need our help, or can we offer ourselves as instruments tuned and ready for Him to play? The Holy Spirit will bring revelation to what we have read and studied. His Word, however, is living, and we can expect new insights even with the most familiar passages. Numerous times I have read a well-known passage, and seen things that I have never seen before.

We are told to study the Word of God, and to be workmen who do not need to be ashamed. Sadly today many Christians are disobedient to that instruction and confine themselves to reading Christian books or short devotionals such as "Word for Today". These are good but no substitute for the Bible itself. Joshua 1:8 records the instruction given through Moses to Joshua,

"Do not let this book of the Law depart from your mouth; meditate on it day and night, so that you may be careful to do everything written in it. Then you will be prosperous and successful."

I have set my heart and mind – my whole being – to live the Word of God. I expect to be instructed, corrected, inspired, challenged, and comforted, to have my questions answered, and to grow daily in understanding of God's person and His ways. It is my life-giving food. Without the manna of God's Word I grow weak, but with it I am daily being changed, my mind is being renewed and my faith is growing. The new-creation man cannot function without His daily bread, "Man shall not live by bread alone, but by every Word that proceeds from the mouth of God."

You may not be a person in public ministry, but everywhere you go you can carry Jesus. I remember reading the story of a muslim lady, Bilquis Sheikh, who had been converted to Jesus, ostracised by her family, and not really knowing how to communicate with them. When her father died, Jesus said, "Carry me to his funeral." She didn't have to say anything, she was carrying the risen Jesus into the heart of hostile territory, and they knew it.

When Peter and John were used by God in the miraculous healing of the man who sat daily at the Beautiful Gate, a large crowd gathered to see what had happened, and Acts 3:12 states,

"Men of Israel, why does this surprise you? Why do you stare at us as if by our own power or godliness we had made this man walk?"

And verse 16 continues,

"It is Jesus' Name and faith that comes through him, that has given this complete healing to him, as you all can see."

Hauled before the religious authorities, in Acts 4:10, Peter, filled with the Holy Spirit, explains,

"It is by the Name of Jesus Christ of Nazareth, whom you crucified but whom God raised from the dead, that this man stands before you healed."

And in verse 13 it says,

"When they saw the courage of Peter and John, and realised that they were unschooled, ordinary men, they were astonished and they took note that these men had been with Jesus."

I would put it in a different way; these 'carriers of Jesus' were letting the risen Jesus continue His works of mercy and power. A little later in Acts 9:34 Peter announces with great confidence,

"Aeneas, Jesus Christ heals you. Get up and take care of your mat".

Jesus may not be visible to the human eye, but His Presence is certainly known by the invisible spirit world. The sons of

Sceva, seeking to deliver a man from demons, used a form of words, but they had no power. Beaten by the demonic presence, they heard these words,

> *"Jesus I know, and I know about Paul, but who are you?" (Acts 19:15)*

I want Jesus to be resident inside me and be manifest through my life. My goal is for him to be seen and heard. As a carrier of Jesus I have been given His Name to use, and His authority. I see His Name as my PIN number to access all of heaven's resources, and His authority given to subdue every vestige of enemy activity aimed either at me, or others, with whom I have contact. Authority is of no use in a latent form. It must be **used** to be effective. Jesus exercised authority over sickness, disease and demons, the weather, and the fish of the sea. Demons are not afraid of you or me, but they tremble at the Name of Jesus, and we need to both know and use this God-given resource.

The prophet Isaiah refers to the coming Messiah as One on whom the Spirit of the Lord is resting,

> *"the Spirit of wisdom, the Spirit of understanding, the Spirit of counsel, the Spirit of power, the Spirit of knowledge, and the Spirit of the fear of the Lord. (Isaiah 11:2-3)*

All these attributes were demonstrated by Jesus, and recorded in the Gospels and the early church. They have been seen in individual heroes of faith throughout the centuries. Today the Holy Spirit is calling forth an army of ordinary men and women who have been with Jesus, who are filled with Jesus in the person of the Holy Spirit, and who expect Jesus to demonstrate His kingdom through them. How dead am I? How alive is Jesus in me? - two questions I ask myself with great regularity.

Charlton Smith worked as a designer for Sanderson's, the wallpaper and fabric company. He was a committed Christian, but a shy man who lived out his faith practically, working with diligence and excellence. However, he did not preach or speak much about Jesus, and he constantly condemned himself for lack of boldness and the fear of man. Believing God was calling him to work full-time for a Christian magazine, he began to pray for his work colleagues, specifically that he would have a meaningful conversation about Jesus with each one before he left the company. That is exactly what happened. He announced he was leaving, and what he was about to do, and in the time remaining he led seven of his colleagues to Jesus. Each time it was they who asked the questions and Jesus in Charlton gave them life-giving answers. The seventh colleague found personal faith in Jesus on Charlton's last day at work. He had learned simply to carry Jesus wherever we went.

Dead men don't react to criticism, to unjust behaviour and the like. There are times when I do, and then I need to go back to the cross, and look again, die again in order to live. In 2 Corinthians 4:10-12, Paul puts it this way,

"We always carry around in our body the death of Jesus, so that the life of Jesus may also be revealed in our body. For we who are alive are always being given over to death for Jesus' sake, so that his life may be revealed in our mortal body. So then death is at work in us, but life is at work in you."

David Hathaway, a man in his 70's who evangelises in Russia and Eastern Europe, seeing thousands of people saved, healed and delivered, recently wrote in his magazine the secrets of his 'success,'

1   Intimate contact with Father God through prevailing
      prayer
2   Faith in the written Word of God

3 Action. An expectation that our 'covenant-keeping God' will demonstrate His power and compassion for helpless, harassed humanity. And the One who is the same yesterday, today and forever, when given the opportunity to work, through ordinary believers, does just that.

If you were to place a coin under a clean piece of paper, and rub over it with a pencil or wax crayon, an image would appear on the paper. A replica of the coin is seen by rubbing. We are being rubbed by life, and what needs to be seen is Jesus, in all His beauty and glory. "Lord, let it be so."

Make it Personal

Romans 12:3b from The Message says,

"Living then, as each one of you does, in pure grace, it's important that you do not misinterpret yourselves as people who are bringing this goodness to God. No. God brings it all to you. The only accurate way to understand ourselves is by what God is and by what he does for us, not by what we are and what we do for him."

1 Thank God for the new life He has given you in Jesus.

2 Everyday expect to see evidence of the resurrection life in what you think, say and how you act.
3 Recall an incident where you know it was Jesus at work and you were simply "carrying him."

Listen to, or download the short message
"Burnt-out Bishops" on www.the222trust.org.uk

Postscript

You have been reading a story of death and resurrection, which has taken many years to unfold and is still continuing. The children of Israel spent 40 years wandering in the desert on a journey that could have taken only 11 days.

I hope you will allow the Holy Spirit to use my story and struggles to enable you to face up your own similar issues, strengthen your faith and bring victory. Each part of your self-life you bring to the cross enables resurrection life to spring forth. In describing some of my own 'memorial stones' my desire is to enable you to speed your journey. In so doing you will grasp the full potential of all that our Father has in mind for you.

I have tried to be totally open and honest, any victories and successes are not due to my own ability, but all thanks must go to my Father and the work of His Holy Spirit.

Books & Resources from Joyce and Charles Sibthorpe

Visit www.the222trust.org.uk

Joyce and Charles also write "Word for the Week"
A new "Word" is posted every Wednesday

Other Books by Joyce Sibthorpe

Can you hear God?   £6.00

God wants to speak to you. He wants you to be able to hear His voice clearly in every situation. You can hear Him if you will take time to listen. This book is full of testimonies and practical examples that will teach you how to hear God's voice.

Is there a Word from the Lord?   £5.99

A sequel, where Joyce expands further on the theme of this book. It will continue to develop your sensitivity in hearing God's voice, and will stretch and stimulate you to keep adventuring with God.

Books by Charles Sibthorpe

Authority   £4.99

We need godly authority in the Church today; this is not acquired simply through knowledge and training, but comes as a result of a calling from God and a living, dynamic relationship with Him. This book speaks to the heart and will challenge every aspect of the life of a leader.

Help Yourself to Health £3.99

If you go to the doctor about your physical condition, he will not only prescribe treatment, but will examine your lifestyle. The same is true spiritually. This book contains practical, Bible based teaching to help release God's healing into every area of your life. It will also provide a check-up to keep you living in a healthy way.

The Bible in one Year £1.00

Read the whole Bible in One Year! Each day you read from the Psalms or Proverbs, the New Testament and the Old Testament. This is a well balanced and interesting way of reading through the Bible regularly and systematically. Needs approx 20 minutes per day.

If you want to Grow £1.00

With this Bible Reading Plan you read the New Testament, Psalms and Proverbs each year and one half of the Old Testament is read the first year and the other half the second year. Well balanced, but takes about two thirds of the time of the One Year Plan.

There are special rates for Churches who want to buy a larger quantity.

You can order these books online at www.the222trust.org.uk
or write to
222 Publications
2 Wrington Road
Congresbury
N Somerset
BS49 5AN